FH4S

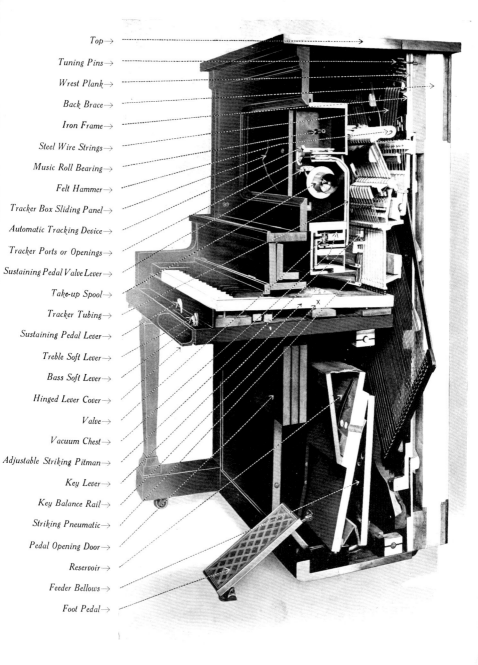

Top→
Tuning Pins→
Wrest Plank→
Back Brace→
Iron Frame→
Steel Wire Strings→
Music Roll Bearing→
Felt Hammer→
Tracker Box Sliding Panel→
Automatic Tracking Device→
Tracker Ports or Openings→
Sustaining Pedal Valve Lever→
Take-up Spool→
Tracker Tubing→
Sustaining Pedal Lever→
Treble Soft Lever→
Bass Soft Lever→
Hinged Lever Cover→
Valve→
Vacuum Chest→
Adjustable Striking Pitman→
Key Lever→
Key Balance Rail→
Striking Pneumatic→
Pedal Opening Door→
Reservoir→
Feeder Bellows→
Foot Pedal→

REBUILDING
THE
PLAYER PIANO

by *LARRY GIVENS*

THE VESTAL PRESS · Vestal, New York

Library of Congress Card Catalog Number 63-15805
ISBN 0-911572-03-1

First Printing 3,000 copies   May 1963
Second Printing 2,000 copies   April 1964
Third Printing 2,000 copies   January 1966
Fourth Printing 3,000 copies   July 1967
Fifth Printing 3,000 copies   June 1969
Sixth Printing 3,000 copies   September 1970
Seventh Printing 3,000 copies   October 1971
Eighth Printing 5,000 copies   November 1972
Ninth Printing 5,000 copies   April 1974
Tenth Printing 5,000 copies   November 1975
Eleventh Printing 5,000 copies   May 1977

INTRODUCTION

TIME WAS in the United States when no home could really be considered complete without its player piano. From the early years of the Twentieth Century to the closing days of the Roaring Twenties, the player piano reigned supreme as the outstanding medium of home entertainment. Many were the parents who scrimped and saved so that their children might know of the finer things in life by having one of these marvelous instruments at their command.

Of course they were really family affairs. The old folks could pedal away at "Annie Laurie" and "Silver Threads Among the Gold" to their hearts content, after the youngsters had had their turn at the William Tell Overture and Paderewski's Minuet. Of course the younger set probably preferred to spend its time with rolls like the "Dill Pickle Rag" and "Moonlight and Roses," but only after they had absorbed their daily quota of culture would mother be likely to permit of such mundane listening.

During World War I when, as in all periods of crisis, entertainment of any variety was at a premium, the player piano

INTRODUCTION

neatly filled this bill by providing an easy means for wafting into the air such tunes as "Roses of Picardy," "My Buddy," "Over There," and "Goodbye Broadway, Hello France." And players helped entertain the boys, too—one well known battleship had six of them on board! And when the boys came back, every player owner felt obliged to rush to his music store for the latest release of "How You Gonna Keep 'em Down on the Farm—(after they've seen Paree?)"

The player was of course not limited to the homes of America. Enterprising men learned early in the game that the public would part with its nickels and dimes to hear these machines located in places of public entertainment, and thus a whole new industry—the nickelodeon business— was formed. No ice cream parlor, pool room, or speakeasy was worthy of public patronage unless standing there, replete with its gaudy stained glass front and repertory of latest hits of the day, was the coin operated piano or orchestrion waiting to grab the customers' nickels.

In the homes of the wealthy, for they were the only people who could afford their rather astronomical price tags, were the reproducing pianos—the players capable of exact re-enactment of the performances of the great artists of the day. At a time when the phonograph was barely capable of capturing and playing back squeaks and squawks, the reproducing piano was able to bring into the home magnificent performances from an actual instrument, right there on the spot, exactly as the artist intended.

With the tremendous advances in technology in recent years, this situation has of course changed. Modern high-fidelity electronic equipment has permitted every home to be a veritable music hall of the highest character. But for

INTRODUCTION

just plain fun, coupled with the nostalgia which Americans in their leisure hours are so fond of seeking, the player piano is simply unequalled.

This book is the first significant attempt to provide the necessary information to bring these fascinating instruments back to life. Mr. Givens is a real expert in these matters, and readers can rest assured that the instructions contained herein are based on much experience. The Vestal Press has taken the lead in re-introducing the player to the American public through its book "Player Piano Treasury" and various catalog reprints, and this volume is a truly significant addition to its publications in this field.

Harvey N. Roehl
April, 1963

PREFACE

THE PURPOSE of this book is to instruct the reader how to rebuild player pianos and related instruments. It is my intent to enable an individual who has had no previous experience in player piano work to do competent rebuilding of most types of roll-operated automatic pianos. This book cannot make an expert repairman out of a person who is unable to change a tire or replace a faucet washer. A certain amount of mechanical ability is essential for player piano work. However, if a reader with a modicum of mechanical ingenuity will follow this book's instructions, he should be able to do a passable job of rebuilding a player piano on his first attempt.

The scope of the book is the *rebuilding* of the player piano, as its title implies. I have not written, nor did I intend to write, a guide to *repairing* the player piano. If the reader expects to find a book full of handy tips for specific, on-the-spot repairing of players, he will be disappointed. This book will not tell "what to do if a Standard Player Action won't track," or "how to fix a stuck valve in an Apollo

PREFACE

player." The only way to learn to do repairing is first to learn to do rebuilding. Therefore, I have attempted to present as clear an account as possible of the processes involved in rebuilding pneumatic player mechanisms. Player pianos, with the exception of the new ones being built today, are "getting old." Many of them have ceased to function because of the deterioration of their pneumatic systems; and those which are still playing on their original systems will eventually need to be rebuilt. As the next decade elapses, fewer and fewer players will still be operating, and more will need rebuilding. I have chosen to concern myself with the complete restoration of the pneumatic actions, rather than with patchwork repairs which may only serve to keep the pianos functioning a little while longer. Any player piano, except the new ones, which is operating thirty years from now will have been *rebuilt*—and it is this facet of the field with which this book deals.

The main focus of the book is on the 88-note upright player piano. In my opinion, any novice should begin his piano-rebuilding career with a simple 88-note pedal player. After he has done several complete jobs on these, he will be ready to advance to more complex instruments such as nickelodeons and reproducing pianos. He should gain his basic, fundamental experience on a few 88-note pedal players before attempting anything else. Pedal players are generally the easiest and least complicated instruments to rebuild; and the novice can be secure in the knowledge that if he should happen to ruin the player mechanism irreparably in his first effort, he has not spoiled a very rare or valuable piece of equipment, as might be the case had he tackled a reproducing piano or a nickelodeon prematurely.

PREFACE

This book contains little material on nickelodeons, and none on band organs and other automatic instruments. Since the book is intended to be an instructor in the basic technique of rebuilding pneumatic player instruments, I see no need to include material on specific types of instruments, with the exception of the reproducing piano. The procedure for re-covering a pneumatic is the same whether the pneumatic happens to come from a nickelodeon, a reproducing piano, an 88-note player, or a band organ. Once the basic procedures of rebuilding are learned, the repairman can take any sort of instrument in his stride. For this reason too, this book does not deal with the rebuilding of each individual make of piano. Not only are there far too many brands to deal with specifically, but it is unnecessary to do so. Anyone can figure out how to take a piano's player action apart: what this book attempts to do is to explain what to do *after* it is apart.

The reproducing piano section, dealing with the Ampico, the Duo-Art, and the Welte-Mignon players, does deal specifically with some of the problems which arise in connection with these instruments. Reproducing pianos are extremely sensitive machines, and certain special techniques are necessary in their adjustment and maintenance. Although reprints of the factory service manuals for the Ampico, the Duo-Art, and the Welte-Mignon are available, they all leave much to the imagination, and often are grossly incomplete. Therefore, the reproducing piano section of this book was written as a supplement to the manuals. There is currently a revival of interest in reproducing pianos, and owing to the scarcity of technicians who are thoroughly conversant with the intricacies of their mechanisms, I

PREFACE

deemed it advisable to include a section dealing with their specific service problems.

The section on reed organ repair is admittedly short; but its length is proportionate to the difficulty of the subject matter. Most reed organs can be repaired easily, and the task is more tedious than difficult. Although reed organs are only remotely related to player pianos, I have included information on their repair because of the increasing number of people who wish to restore old organs for use in homes. Since the techniques of repairing organs are not too much different from those of repairing player pianos, it seemed apropos to include them here.

It is highly recommended that entire sections of the book be read at one time. This is advantageous not only in that the reader can carry his train of thought to its conclusion, but also because of the nature of the material presented. Technical material is difficult to compress; and, due to the mechanics of literary presentation, one occasionally has to get ahead of oneself, so to speak. When describing, in detail, the procedure of performing a certain operation, it is not always possible to present the various steps in order. Occasionally, an operation must be begun before the previous one is completed—yet the instructional material would become incoherent if presented in this manner. For this reason, it is wise to read an entire section through to get the general picture of what must be done, before starting to do the described work.

Since this is the first publication dealing with player piano rebuilding which approaches book length, I have had no predecessors on whom to build or to enlarge. As is generally the case with "firsts" in any field, this book will probably be

PREFACE

criticized as incomplete or inadequate in certain sections of its subject matter. In defense of this criticism, I can only say that the book has been written solely from my personal experience as a collector and restorer of automatic pianos. If my experience has been somewhat one-sided in any aspects of the field, I have no doubt that it will show up in this book. However, one has to begin somewhere; and the need for a technical treatise on rebuilding the player piano is presently so great that this book, adequate or not, will, I hope, perform its intended service.

I am grateful to the individuals who have encouraged and assisted my efforts. In particular, I wish to thank Durrell Armstrong, Roy Haning, and Harvey Roehl for their contributions of needed information and advice.

LARRY GIVENS
January, 1963

TABLE OF CONTENTS

HOW IT WORKS

BEFORE BEGINNING to discuss the technique of rebuilding the player piano, it may be well to give the reader a brief illustrated outline of its operation. An understanding of how the player piano works—what makes it play—is essential for a repairman who expects to produce a good job.

The player piano operates using vacuum, or suction, as its motive power. In most players, the vacuum is created by pedaling with the feet, which operates suction bellows in the lower portion of the piano. This vacuum is channeled through large supply hoses into the upper action of the piano, where it does the work of playing the keys.

Probably the most important parts of the player piano are its valves and pneumatics. These parts utilize the vacuum and actuate the piano's notes. Each note has its individual valve and pneumatic unit. The valve controls the suction which collapses the pneumatic on cue from the music roll. The pneumatic, which is nothing more than a small bellows with a push-rod attached, operates its piano note by suddenly collapsing, due to the rapid admission of vacuum to its interior. The note strikes with a loudness

1

which is proportional to the degree of suction which actuates its pneumatic.

Figure 1 is a drawing of a typical valve and pneumatic unit, in schematic form. The tube A leads from the suction supply bellows, and provides motive power to actuate the valve B and collapse the pneumatic C. Tube D leads from the tracker bar (the brass or wooden bar over which the music roll plays). When a perforation in the music roll passes over the tracker bar, air is admitted through tube D. This air allows the pouch E (a flexible diaphragm of very thin leather) to rise, due to the vacuum above it. Pouch E, in rising, carries with it the valve B, lifting the valve away from its lower seat and throwing it upwards against its upper seat. This seals off the hole in the upper valve seat, and allows vacuum to rush up past the valve stem through the hole in the lower valve seat, and into the pneumatic C. Thus the pneumatic collapses, and pushes rod F upwards which plays a note on the piano. When the perforation passes away from the tracker bar, the tube D is once again sealed off, and vacuum is admitted to the chamber underneath the pouch E through the small hole G, called the bleed (usually a small stamped brass cup with a hole in its base). Atmospheric pressure on top of the valve B forces the valve downward onto its lower seat. This seals off the suction supply to the pneumatic C, and allows atmosphere to rush into the pneumatic through the hole in the upper valve seat, thus opening the pneumatic again.

Figure 2 is an actual cross section of the modern Pianola, reproduced by permission of the Hardman-Peck Company, its manufacturer. Note that it operates on the single-valve principle.

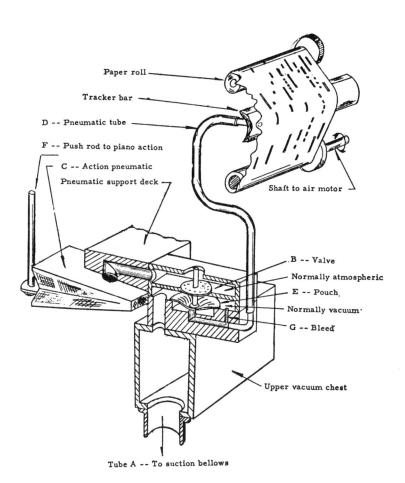

Fig. 1. Single Valve Pneumatic System

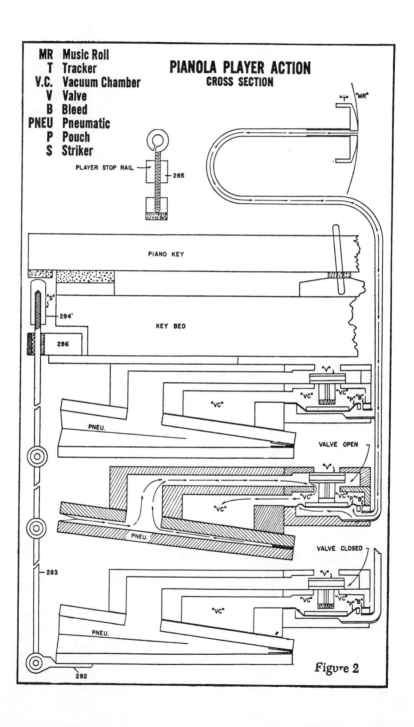

Figure 2

HOW IT WORKS

A variation on this mechanism is found in pianos which are built with a double-valve action. In this case, two valves per note are used. The first, or primary, valve actuates the main, or secondary, valve, which operates the pneumatic in normal fashion. Figure 3 is a drawing of a typical double-valve action. The two tubes A are suction supply tubes. Tube B leads from the tracker bar. When a note perforation

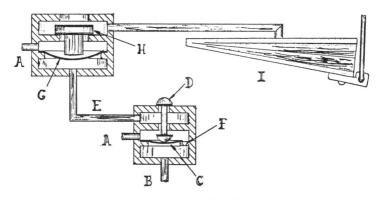

Fig. 3. A Typical Double-valve Action

A—Suction supply
B—Tube from tracker bar
C—Primary pouch
D—Primary valve
E—Channel from primary to
    secondary valve
F—Primary bleed
G—Secondary pouch
H—Secondary valve
I—Pneumatic

opens the tracker bar hole, primary pouch C rises, lifting primary valve D. As the valve moves, its top part is lifted away from the upper valve seat, admitting atmosphere into channel E. At the same time the lower part of the valve is thrown against the lower seat, shutting off vacuum to channel E. The effect of this is to admit atmosphere to the chamber beneath the secondary valve pouch G, causing

5

it to rise and to throw secondary valve H against its upper seat, closing off atmosphere to pneumatic I and admitting suction to it. Thus the pneumatic closes. When the perforation passes away from the tracker bar, the bleed F restores the vacuum beneath the primary pouch C, the primary valve D drops to its rest position, and atmosphere in tube E is sealed off. Vacuum is admitted to tube E, and this pulls secondary pouch G down again, allowing secondary valve H to drop to its position of rest and admit atmosphere to pneumatic I, causing it to open. In the double-valve player action, the secondary valve has no bleed, as the secondary pouch is pulled down to its rest position by vacuum from the primary valve, thus making a secondary bleed unnecessary.

The air-motor provides motive power for the music roll. This air-motor is nothing more than a series of bellows connected to a crankshaft in such fashion that the bellows collapse in a certain order when vacuum is alternately admitted and shut off by a series of eccentric-driven sliding valves, causing the crankshaft to rotate. The vacuum supply to the air-motor is channeled through a governing device which assures constant speed of the air-motor regardless of what vacuum may be present in the main supply bellows (i. e., regardless of how hard the player pianist pumps the pedals). Different types of governors are found in player pianos, but the basic principle of their operation is always the same. They control the flow of vacuum to the air-motor, thus controlling its speed. The governor is usually a fairly large pneumatic, through which the vacuum supply to the air-motor flows. Inside this pneumatic is some sort of "strangling" device, usually a sliding valve made of wood

HOW IT WORKS

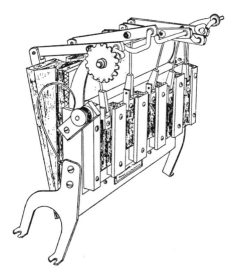

Fig. 4. An Air-motor

or metal—see Figure 5. A spring attached to the pneumatic exerts constant force on it, tending to keep it open at all times. As the player pianist pumps, the suction to the air-motor flows into the governor pneumatic through a supply hose, and out again through another hose, after passing through the sliding valve inside the pneumatic. This suction tends to partially collapse the pneumatic, against the force of the spring. This collapsing of the pneumatic moves the sliding valve's position, and partially constricts the flow of suction through the pneumatic. If the player pianist pumps harder, the air-motor would naturally tend to speed up, due to higher vacuum turning it. However, in this case the governor pneumatic collapses farther, moving the sliding valve so that it closes off the suction supply opening still more, thus reducing the supply of suction to the air-

7

motor in proportion to the increase in the main supply bellows suction. If the player pianist pumps lightly, this would normally cause the air-motor to slow down—but the governor pneumatic expands, opening the sliding valve and allowing more suction to flow. In this way the suction to the

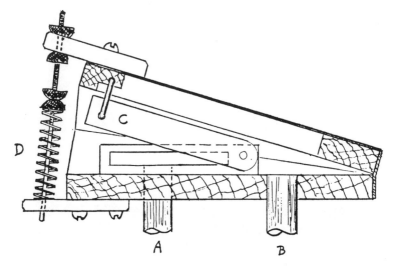

Fig. 5. An Air-motor Governor Unit

A—Channel from suction supply   C—Sliding valve
B—Channel to air motor   D—Adjustable spring

air-motor is always kept constant, regardless of the level of the supply vacuum.

Usually attached to the governor pneumatic is the tempo regulation device, which is simply a sliding valve which partially shuts off the flow of regulated suction, after it has passed through the governor, which operates the air-motor. The position of the sliding valve is determined by the tempo lever. If the music roll being played runs at a high tempo,

8

the lever is set to the prescribed position on the tempo indicator. This moves the sliding valve such that it allows most of the suction to reach the air-motor. If the tempo lever is set to a low value, little of the suction is allowed to reach the air-motor, thus moving the roll at a slow speed.

When the piano is rewinding, the action cutoff valve shuts off the flow of suction to the upper player action, thus preventing the piano from operating. In foot-powered player pianos, these cutoff valves are usually mechanically operated from the rewind-play lever, although occasionally a pneumatically-operated cutoff is found. Another valve opens a channel which bypasses the governor pneumatic, making the air-motor rewind the roll at a high speed.

The apparatus in the lower part of the piano supplies the necessary suction to operate the player mechanism. Each foot pedal has its own pump bellows, to which it is connected by linkage. When a pedal is pressed, one of the pumps opens, drawing air from the pneumatic stack into it. When the pedal is released, the air with which the pump has filled itself is expelled into the atmosphere. This is accomplished by two simple valves, usually in the form of flaps of leather, which act as check valves to control the direction of flow of the air. Figure 6 is an illustration of the principle of operation of the pumps. A represents the fixed board of the pump, and B represents the movable board, attached through linkage to the foot pedal. Channel C leads through the reservoir to the player action. The leather flap valves D are attached to the boards at their ends, but are free to move away from the boards at their centers. When the pedal is pressed and the pump opens, valve D on the movable board is drawn tightly against its seat, while valve D on the fixed board is pulled away from its seat, drawing air from channel C. When the pedal is released, the pump has filled itself with air from channel C, and it begins to close. Valve D on the fixed board is then pressed against its seat, while

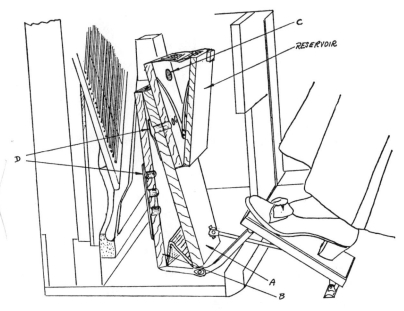

Fig. 6. Main Pump Bellows

A—Fixed Deck   C—Channel to player action
B—Movable deck   D—Leather flap valves

valve D on the movable board moves away from its seat, expelling the air in the pump into the atmosphere.

The reservoir acts as a cushioner and equalizer for the supply of air. The two foot pump bellows supply vacuum only while they are being pushed open, and this would lead to very erratic performance of the piano if there were no means to smooth out the vacuum supply and assure a reasonably constant suction. The reservoir is a large spring-loaded bellows which "stores" the generated suction inside it. When the piano is playing, the reservoir is partially collapsed. The movable board of the reservoir is in a continually "floating" state, moving in and out quickly as variations in suction occur. If a heavy chord is struck, the reservoir springs snap the movable board out instantaneously to maintain the working vacuum and to keep the piano playing normally. Pianos with small reservoirs usually give the player pianist better opportunity to accent certain notes by quick, hard strokes of the pedals. However, pianos with large reservoirs usually maintain their playing level more uniformly and are better able to handle sudden demands for vacuum. Some player pianos are equipped with two reservoir bellows at the ends of the bellows unit, rather than a single reservoir extending across the unit—but the function is the same in both cases.

The rest of the player piano's mechanism is comparatively simple. The roll drive transmission shifts the control gears from rewind to play position as determined by the control lever. The automatic tracking device shifts the position of the roll to see that its perforations are always in direct alignment with the holes in the tracker bar. Some automatic trackers shift only the upper spool, some shift the tracker bar, and some shift both the upper and lower spools, but their operation is basically the same. Most player pianos are equipped with various "interpretive" devices whereby the operator can make the piano play at different loudness levels at his discretion. These devices are controlled from levers or push-buttons which are located on the control rail in front of the key-bed. These so-called expression controls were

11

manufactured in literally dozens of forms, and any general description of them would be impossible. However, they all operate by causing the bass and treble sections of the hammer rail to move closer to the strings, or by "strangling" the suction supply to the player action in much the same fashion as the air-motor governor operates.

Many player pianos came equipped with an automatic device for operating the sustaining pedal. This consists of a large pneumatic which is connected to the sustaining pedal mechanism, and which is controlled either by a push-button or lever on the control rail or by a special sustaining pedal perforation cut into most music rolls. This pneumatic actuates the sustaining pedal when the finger button is pushed or when the pedal perforation crosses the tracker bar, the result being the lifting of the dampers from the strings, just as though the regular sustaining pedal had been pressed.

REBUILDING

BEFORE ANY PARTS of the mechanical action can be removed from the piano, the removable case parts must be taken off the front of the instrument. Remove the upper front panel of the piano by lifting it from its brackets or by turning thumb nuts and raising it off its mounting screws. Remove the flat board, if any, above the fallboard, and also the fallboard itself. On some pianos, the two vertical pieces of wood at the two ends of the front of the piano must be removed to allow the upper player action to come out. The bottom front panel should also be removed—and in some cases it is helpful to remove the piano's top, especially if it is a small player.

The player action, or pneumatic stack, is removed from the piano by loosening the control rods at the ends of the action, detaching the air-motor supply hose, removing the bolts or screws at the ends of the action which hold it in place, and then lifting the action outward from the back of the piano and slightly upward at the same time. This procedure may vary with some pianos which have the large vacuum supply hoses attached to the action beneath one or both ends: naturally, these must be removed before lifting the action out of the piano. Occasionally pianos have supporting brackets which run from the top of the player action back to the iron frame, and these must be detached. Pianos which have an automatic sustaining pedal will be equipped with a tube leading from the spool box to the left end of the player action, thence to the bottom of the piano, and this should be disconnected.

The lower bellows may be removed from the piano by loosening the screws or bolts which hold the bellows in place, and by lifting the entire unit out of the bottom of the piano. Generally the control rod linkage must be disconnected before the unit can be removed. If the suction supply hose for the automatic sustaining pedal pneumatic runs directly from the bellows unit, it should be removed before the unit is lifted out. Different piano manufacturers varied the structure of their pianos greatly, and any general description of the methods of anchoring units in place or of placement of component parts would be virtually impossible.

All the "accessory" devices, such as the automatic sustaining pedal pneumatic, the expression pneumatics which operate sections of the hammer rail, and any other such mechanisms, should be removed from the piano at this time.

The reader may think it odd that the first step in doing the work on a player piano should involve not the player action, but the piano itself—yet this is indeed the case. This writer strongly recommends that as soon as the repairman has removed all the player mechanism from his piano, he should set the mechanism aside and turn his attention to the piano itself. It is an undeniable fact that any player is only as good as the *piano* in which it is installed. A perfectly-operating player mechanism cannot give satisfactory musical results if it is coupled to a piano which is in need of attention.

It is not the province of this book to attempt to instruct the repairman in making the necessary adjustments and repairs to the piano action and frame. Suffice it to say that the piano action should be carefully inspected for lost motion and wear in bushings, the hammer butts should be checked for clicking noises, looseness, and sloppy travel, and the backcheck and let-off adjustments should be regulated if necessary. Bridle straps should be replaced if they are worn or broken. All felt parts should be checked for moth damage. The hammers should be dressed, if necessary, to remove grooves cut in their felt by the strings. The sounding-board should be checked, and if it is badly cracked it should be repaired. The piano should be tuned while the player action is removed and the action and strings are accessible. If new bass strings are necessary to replace ones on which the windings have loosened, they should be installed at this time. If the player mechanic does not wish to do this work himself, a qualified piano technician can undertake this part of the job. But the fact should never be forgotten that unless the piano itself is in top condition, the repairman is wasting his time on the player action, for the musical results can only be unsatisfactory.

Figures 7 (a, b, and c) are included here merely for the purpose of giving the inexperienced repairman an opportunity to identify the parts of a piano action.

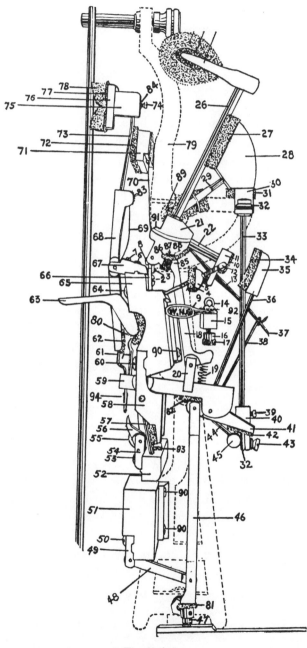

Fig. 7 (a)

DIAGRAM OF UPRIGHT PIANO ACTION
Sectional View

1 Upr. Spoon.

2 Upr. Brass Flange Rail Screw.

3 Upr. Brass Rail Plate.

4 Upr. Block Rail Felt.

5 Upr. Block Rail.

6 Upr. Damper Flange Screw.

7 Upr. Damper Spring Reg. Screw.

8 Upr. Brass Rail Plate Screw.

9 Upr. Regulating Rail Bracket.

10 Upr. Butt Chack (Buckskin) Covering.

11 Upr. Butt Check.

12 Upr. Right & Left Regulating Screw for Block Rail.

13 Upr. Bridle.

14 Upr. Regulating Screw.

15 Upr. Regulating Rail.

16 Upr. Regulating Button.

17 Upr. Regulating Button Punching.

18 Upr. Jack.

19 Upr. Jack Spring.

20 Upr. Jack Flange.

21 Upr. Butt

22 Upr. Butt Shank.

23 Upr. Hammer Felt.

24 Upr. Hammer Underfelt.

25 Upr. Hammer Head.

26 Upr. Hammer Shank.

27 Upr. Hammer Rail Cloth.

28 Upr. Hammer Rail.

29 Upr. Hammer Rail Hook.

30 Upr. L. M. P. Top Piece.

31 Upr. Hammer Rail Block Felt.

32 Upr. L. M. P. Rubber Bushing.

33 Upr. L. M. P. Connecting Pin.

34 Upr. Backcheck Felt.

35 Upr. Backcheck.

36 Upr. Backcheck Wire.

37 Upr. Bridle Leather Tip.

38 Upr. Bridle Wire.

39 Upr L. M. P. Set Screw.

40 Upr. L. M. P. Bottom Pin.

41 Upr. L. M. P. Lever.

42 Upr. L. M. P. Cloth.

43 Upr. L. M. P. Rod Screw.

44 Upr. L. M. P. Rod Hook.

45 Upr. L. M. P. Rod.

46 Upr. Extension.

47 Upr. Capstan Screw.

48 Upr. Extension Guide

49 Upr. Guide Flange.

Fig. 7 (b)

50 Upr. Guide Flange Screw.

51 Upr. Extension Rail.

52 Upr. Sostenuto Rail.

53 Upr. Sostenuto Flange Screw

54 Upr. Sostenuto Flange.

55 Upr. Sostenuto Lever Spring.

56 Upr. Sostenuto Lever.

57 Upr. Sostenuto Rail Hook.

58 Upr. Sostenuto Hook Flange.

59 Upr. Wippen.

60 Upr. Wippen Flange Screw.

61 Upr. Sostenuto Wire.

62 Upr. Damper Lever Cloth.

63 Upr. Damper Rod.

64 Upr. Damper Rod Hinge.

65 Upr. Main Rail.

66 Upr. Brass Rail.

67 Upr. Damper Flange.

68 Upr. Damper Lever.

69 Upr. Damper Spring.

70 Upr. Spring Rail Spring.

71 Upr. Spring Rail.

72 Upr. Spring Rail Felt.

73 Upr. Damper Wire.

74 Upr. Damper Block Screw.

75 Upr. Damper Block.

76 Upr. Bass Damper Plate.

77 Upr. Damper Undercovering.

78 Upr. Damper Felt.

79 Upr. Bracket.

80 Upr. Damper Rod Felt Cushion.

81 Upr. Extension Cloth.

82 Upr. L. M. P. Wippen Cloth.

83 Upr. Damper Lever Punching.

84 Upr. Brass Damper Block Studs.

85 Upr. Butt Felt.

86 Upr. Butt Leather.

87 Upr. Butt (Scarlet) Undercovering Cloth.

88 Upr. Butt (White) Undercovering Cloth.

89 Upr. Bracket Bushing Cloth.

90 Upr. Bracket Screw.

91 Upr. Butt Punching Cloth.

92 Upr. Regulating Bracket Punching Leather.

93 Upr. Sostenuto Lever Felt.

94 Upr. Sostenuto Wire Cloth.

The action from which this diagram was made is a WESSELL, NICKEL & GROSS model.

Fig. 7 (c)

To be discussed at this point is the operation of overhauling and rebuilding the upper action, or pneumatic stack, of the player piano—probably the most important part of the entire job. The pneumatic stack contains delicate, precision parts. Unless these parts are handled and rebuilt with care, the results will be disappointing.

The first step in rebuilding the stack is separating it into

18

its upper and lower parts. The stack is examined to see where the "break" is located, then separated. Usually the two parts separate at a point near the lower ends of the tubing which runs from the tracker bar into the action, just above the top row of pneumatics. On some actions, this tracker bar tubing may have to be detached at its lower ends before the parts will separate. Examination will determine this. Some ingenuity may be required, as manufacturers' practices varied to such an extent that it is impossible to give any general procedure for this operation.

When the two sections are apart, the upper half should be set aside and work on the pneumatics should be begun.

On many player actions, the decks to which the pneumatics are glued are fastened together by long screws which pass through the junction areas at the ends of the stack, or else by metal brackets outside the ends of the stack. On others, the decks are screwed onto a board which supports all the decks at once. In the latter case, access to the screws which hold the decks to the main board is gained by removing the screwed-on board on the front face of the stack. The screws are in the chamber beneath this board. Occasionally the decks are glued to the supporting board, and must be carefully worked off with a putty-knife and mallet. In any case, examination of the stack will enable the repairman to discover its structure.

Unscrew or otherwise loosen the decks from the supporting body, but do not attempt to remove them from their approximate position.

After all the decks have been loosened, turn the stack upside down, with the pneumatics facing you. Remove the screws from the individual pneumatics' push-rod brackets

and break the brackets free from the bottom of the pneumatics (see Figure 8). Do the uppermost deck first, and
after all the brackets have been detached from the pneumatics the deck will be free and can be lifted away from
the remaining decks. Care should be taken to number or

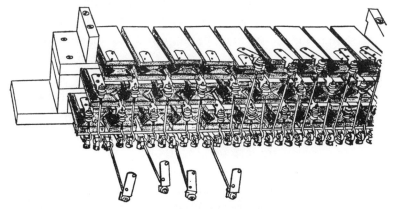

Fig. 8. Removal of Push-rod Brackets

otherwise identify the decks so that they can be replaced
in their proper order when the action is reassembled.

Use the same procedure to free the remaining decks, and
when the last deck is freed of its push-rods, the long rail
holding the push-rod guides should be removed from the
top side of the deck, if it is removable. The screws which
hold the push-rod brackets to the pneumatics should be
put in a small container and placed where they will not be
disturbed.

The individual pneumatics should now be removed from
the decks, in preparation for recovering them. With a soft
pencil or ball-point pen, mark each pneumatic on each deck
such that it can be replaced in its proper position when the

decks are reassembled. Number or letter each pneumatic consecutively, using a different identification system for each deck, to prevent confusion later. Make a mark on the end of each deck to indicate where the identification system

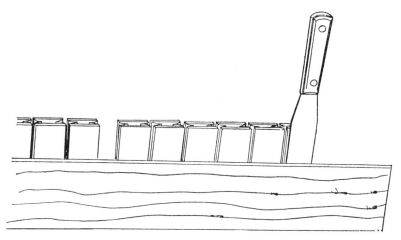

Fig. 9. Removal of Pneumatics from Deck

begins, to prevent replacing the pneumatics in reverse order during re-assembly.

After the marking is completed, the pneumatics should be removed from the decks. This is done by gently driving a thin putty-knife or other flat-bladed instrument between each pneumatic and the deck. Most pneumatics were originally attached to the decks with animal glue, which is brittle enough to make them removable without much damage. Stand the decks on edge on the workbench, and gently drive the blade into the point (see Figure 9). Be sure that the blade enters the joint completely parallel with the two mated surfaces, to prevent its digging into the wood. Use a

21

wooden mallet or other non-metallic hammer, and be gentle. Most pneumatics will pop off the decks without trouble after a few taps of the mallet. Occasionally, however, pneumatics in which the wood grain runs at an angle with the deck will begin to split, rather than come off the deck freely. When this occurs, turn the deck over and begin driving the blade into the joint from the other end, or from the side of the pneumatic, if it is accessible. With a little care and patience, all the pneumatics can be removed from the decks in this fashion. An extremely stubborn pneumatic can be removed by heating the inner surface of the pneumatic. Tear the old cloth off the boards and lay the movable board of the pneumatic back out of the way. Lay a hot iron on the top board of the pneumatic, and in a short time the heat will penetrate to the glued joint and soften it somewhat, aiding in its removal. In case a pneumatic has split badly in coming off its deck, put a little glue on the surfaces of the split and secure it with a small clamp, taking care to wipe away all glue which squeezes out. The decks can now be set aside until the pneumatics have been re-covered. *Do not* plane or otherwise attempt to smooth off the surfaces of the decks from which the pneumatics have been removed. Leave them just as they are—for the pneumatics must later be glued back onto the decks in the exact position from which they were removed, and any disturbance of the mating surfaces of the deck or pneumatic will result in a weakened joint.

The span of the pneumatics should be measured and noted. With a ruler, measure the span of cloth covering the open end of one of the pneumatics, including the boards (see Figure 10). Be sure to stretch the pneumatic open to

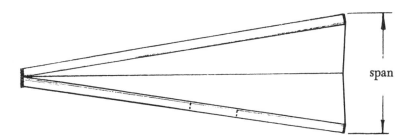

Fig. 10. Measuring the Span of a Pneumatic, with the Old Cloth
Stretched Tight

its fullest extent while doing this. This measurement will determine the width of the new strips of cloth which will be
glued on.

The pneumatics should now be cleaned. There are a number of methods by which this can be done, but for purposes
of illustration the power sander will be used. This writer has
found the sander to be by far the most satisfactory method.

If a combination disc and belt table sander is available,
this is the ideal tool for cleaning the pneumatics. Figure 11

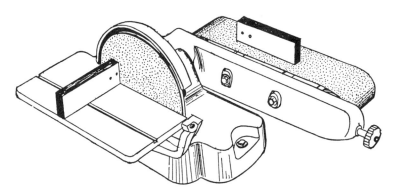

Fig. 11. Cleaning the Old Cloth from a Pneumatic

illustrates the position of the pneumatics on the sander. The two sides of each pneumatic are first cleaned on the sanding belt. Then the ends of each pneumatic are cleaned on the disc. The disc table insures that the cleaned ends will be perpendicular to the sides of the pneumatic, and prevents distortion of the pneumatic's shape. The hinge end of each pneumatic should be pressed lightly against the sanding disc, to prevent sanding into the cloth hinge. This hinge end does not necessarily need to be cleaned down to the bare wood, as this might endanger the hinge. The other three sides, however, should be sanded down to clean wood. Coarse sandpaper should be used. The old pneumatic cloth does not need to be removed before cleaning, as the sandpaper will quickly cut through the dead cloth, and the folded piece in the interior of the pneumatic can be plucked out and discarded.

If a combination sander is not available, a separate disc sander or belt sander can be used, providing care is taken to sand the pneumatics' surfaces evenly and not to distort their shape. If no sander of any type is available, the pneumatics can be cleaned by clamping them in a bench vise and cleaning their surfaces with a hand plane, preferably one of the surface-forming type. The pneumatics must be turned in the vise to clean all four edges.

The strips of pneumatic cloth should now be made. Only the thinnest cloth should be used to cover the stack pneumatics, as they must be perfectly flexible and should offer no resistance to movement. With a pocket tape measure, determine the perimeter of the outer surfaces of one of the pneumatics. All four surfaces must be totaled to determine the perimeter. Add approximately a quarter of an inch for overlapping cloth at the hinge end of the pneumatics, and this will determine the length of the new cloth strips. The width of the strip is determined by the span of the pneumatics, which was measured before they were cleaned. Lay the large uncut piece of pneumatic cloth on a flat surface, and square off any raggedness on its end. Measure back from the end of the cloth the distance which was determined to be the length of the strips. Draw a straight line across the cloth parallel to its end, on the white side of the cloth. Then, cut the cloth along this line with sharp scissors. Figure 12 shows the pattern of the cloth. With the measuring tape or

Fig. 12. Cutting Pneumatic Cloth into Strips. It may also be Torn to Size, as indicated in the Text.

yardstick, measure along the cut edge and make a series of small pencil marks at intervals which mark the span of the pneumatics. Then, cut small nicks in the edge of the cloth at these marks. The pneumatic cloth can then be smoothly torn into strips, using the scissor nicks as "starters" for each strip. Repeat the above operation until enough strips to do the entire set of pneumatics have been made.

Pneumatic cloth strips can be torn, rather than cut, and this saves much time. However, it should always be remembered that the cloth can be torn only along its length as it comes from the supplier. The weave of the cloth runs parallel to its edges, and it will tear uniformly along that dimension. If one attempts to tear the cloth cross-wise—i. e., across the strip from edge to edge—the result will be crooked strips which will be useless. Always lay out the strip pattern along the length of the cloth, as shown in Figure 12.

To be discussed at this point is the procedure for covering the pneumatics. *Heed it well!* The repairman should remember that this same basic procedure applies when bellows of *any* size or shape are covered. Throughout any player piano are dozens, often hundreds, of bellows large and small— each of which is covered using this same method. This procedure should become a habit, and the repairman should eventually be able to do it blindfolded, so to speak.

The pneumatics are covered, naturally, one at a time. Lay a strip of pneumatic cloth on a smooth surface with the rubber side down. Spread a layer of glue on the open end of the pneumatic. Place the glued surfaces of the pneumatic on the edges of the center of the strip of cloth. Rock the pneumatic back and forth crosswise to press the entire surface of each board down tightly against the cloth—being careful, at the same time, not to shift the boards' position on the edges of the cloth. Figure 13 shows the position of the pneumatic when this step is completed.

Lay the pneumatic on one side, folding the lower side of the strip of cloth back underneath the pneumatic and pull-

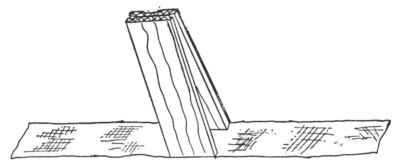

Fig. 13. The First Step in Gluing a Pneumatic

ing it snug to prevent it from loosening where it has already been glued. Spread glue on the uppermost side surfaces of the pneumatic. Taking care to see that the cloth is pulled tight to insure its coming down onto the boards evenly, lay the cloth down on the boards and press it firmly against them with the fingers. Figure 14 illustrates this step completed.

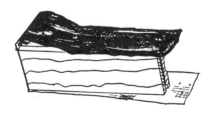

Fig. 14. The Second Step in Gluing a Pneumatic

27

Turn the pneumatic onto its other side, and do the same thing, as shown in Figure 15. Always remember to keep the cloth tight as it is laid onto the boards, as this will prevent any buckling or looseness at the corners of the pneumatic.

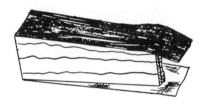

Fig. 15. The Third Step in Gluing a Pneumatic

Stand the pneumatic on end. If the cloth has been properly centered, the two portions which fold over onto the hinge end should be approximately equal.

Spread glue onto the hinge end of the pneumatic. Fold one end of the cloth down onto the board and press very lightly. Then lift this end back up off the board, and fold the other end down quickly. Press the second end down tightly onto the board—and then fold the first end over again and press it down firmly. In this way, the first end which is pressed onto the board picks up a supply of glue, and is then lifted off. The second end is then glued down; and the first end, which already has glue on it, is pressed on. This procedure eliminates the tedious and messy job of spreading the glue onto the cloth ends, and it is by far the fastest method of processing the hinge end of pneumatics of any type. Figure 16 shows the pneumatic after the cloth has been glued onto all four sides.

A word about application of the glue should be inserted

here. If the repairman elects to use hot glue, he will, of course, apply it with a brush. However, if he employs any of the white glues, or other non-heated glue, he will experience difficulty in spreading an even layer on the pneumatics and

Fig. 16. The Fourth Step in Gluing a Pneumatic

other parts if he attempts to remain fastidiously clean. The best spreader for glue which has ever been discovered is the *finger*, pure and simple! No repairman has ever rebuilt a player action without getting his hands dirty; and whatever glue sticks to the fingers can be easily removed with hot water and soap.

When glue is applied to the edges of the stack pneumatics and other parts of the action, it should be spread evenly in a layer just thick enough to conceal the surface beneath it, yet not so thick that it will begin to form runs if the surface is raised to a vertical position. When the cloth is pressed onto the pneumatic boards, only a little glue should squeeze out from the joints. If no glue at all shows, probably an insufficient quantity is being used—and if the glue squeezes out in abundance, too much is being applied. Large pneumatics will require a somewhat thicker layer of glue. A little practice will enable the repairman to judge this as he applies the glue.

After the pneumatics have been covered and have dried for at least an hour, they must be trimmed. This is done using a sharp scissors, preferably long-bladed ones which can trim an entire side of a pneumatic in one bite. Place the scissors such that the interior surface of one of the blades is flat against the wooden board of the pneumatic. Cut the cloth perfectly flush with the wood. Figure 17 illustrates the scissors position and the method of procedure. Trim all the edges on one board, then trim the other board, and proceed to do the entire set in this manner.

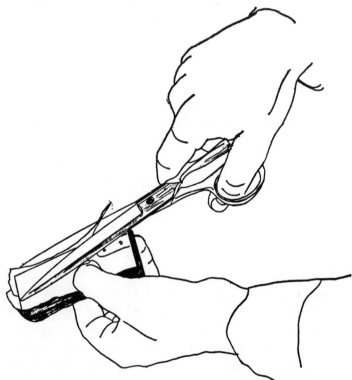

Fig. 17. Trimming a Pneumatic

REBUILDING

The pneumatics should then be creased. This is done by holding each pneumatic completely open, and placing the thumb and middle finger on the cloth near the open end. With the forefinger, press the cloth covering the open end

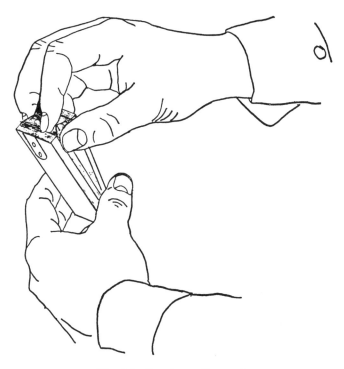

Fig. 18. Creasing a Pneumatic

of the pneumatic downward, back into the pneumatic, as shown in Figure 18. Keeping the cloth in this position, close the pneumatic and squeeze it tightly, which will impart a permanent crease to the cloth.

The pneumatics are now ready to be glued back onto their respective decks. The pneumatics for a single deck are laid out on the workbench in their consecutive numbered or lettered order. The deck is also placed on the bench in front of the pneumatics in its proper position to receive them. Glue is spread onto the mating surface of the deck, and the pneumatics are placed in their respective positions consecutively. This operation is an important one, and the repairman must take care to replace the pneumatics in exactly their former position, with the mating surfaces completely joined. Usually, the repairman can feel the pneumatic slip into its proper place, if the mating surfaces have not been tampered with.

When re-attaching pneumatics to the decks, large spring-type clamps should be used. The repairman should equip himself with at least half a dozen of these, preferably with a throat of three inches or more. Figure 19 illustrates the type

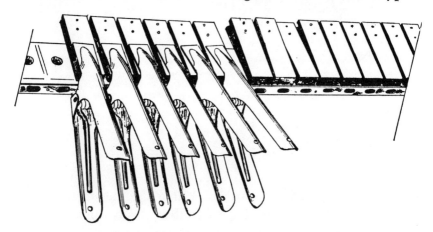

Fig. 19. Re-gluing Pneumatics to a Deck

of clamp required. For re-attaching the pneumatics to their decks, hot glue should be used. After the glue has been applied to the deck and the pneumatic has been pressed into its position, a clamp should be quickly put on to hold the pneumatic under pressure. This should be done in consecutive order, without removing the preceding clamps. When the repairman has used his seventh or eighth clamp, the glue under the first pneumatic will be sufficiently set so that he can remove the clamp from the first pneumatic and use it over again. In this way the repairman can proceed down the line of pneumatics, attaching all of them without interruption. This procedure is usable only with hot glue. White glue must be left under pressure for several hours before the clamps may be removed, and for this reason its use for re-attaching pneumatics is not suggested. Also, the repairman should consider the situation of the person who may be rebuilding the piano again, thirty or forty years hence. It is considerably easier to remove pneumatics which have been attached with hot glue than those on which white glue has been used.

While the pneumatics are drying on the decks, the repairman may turn his attention to the remainder of the lower portion of the stack, containing the valves, pouches, and bleeds. Proper operation of these parts is essential to a well-running player piano.

Ideally, every valve in the pneumatic stack should be inspected and cleaned. Naturally, they must be removed from the stack for this operation. The location and positioning of the valves in player actions differs so widely from maker to

maker that any generalization would be useless. The repairman must use his ingenuity in locating the valves and in
determining how to remove them.

Figure 20 illustrates one fairly common method of valve
positioning. The view shows the front side of the lower part

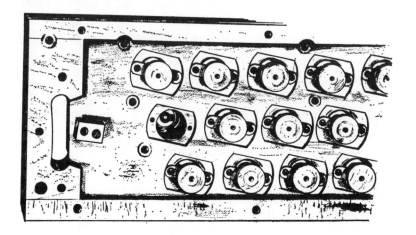

Fig. 20. A Valve Deck with One Valve Removed

of the stack with the long screwed-on pouch board removed.
The valves in this type of action travel horizontally. They
are removed by unscrewing the wood screws fastening the
metal valve seat to the valve deck, and then slipping the
valves out frontwards. One valve is shown removed from
the stack. The wooden knobs on the front end of the valve

stems merely prevent the pouches from being pierced by the end of the stems.

Figure 21 shows valves of the so called "unit block" type. These unit blocks, which contain the pouch, valve, and bleed, unscrew separately from the front of the pneumatic stack, which makes service on them quite easy. They are found in

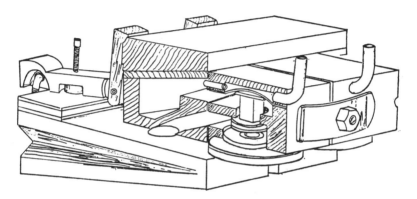

Fig. 21. The Unit-block Type of Valve, as Manufactured by the Amphion Action Company

both upright and inverted styles; the ones in the drawing, with the pouches above the valve, are of the inverted type.

Occasionally the pouches, valves, and bleeds are built into the top of the individual pneumatics. Figure 22 illustrates one of these. Some manufacturers built the valve-pouch-bleed assembly directly into the pneumatic decks. In any case, the repairman must examine the stack to determine the method of construction, and thus the method of removal, of the valves.

The valves should be removed one by one, and their fac-

35

ing surfaces brushed with a stiff brush. An old toothbrush is ideal for this purpose. The valves must be replaced in the same units from which they came, so the repairman should remove only one at a time, clean it, and replace it. Every particle of dirt must be removed from the valve facings, and the seats should also be cleaned if necessary.

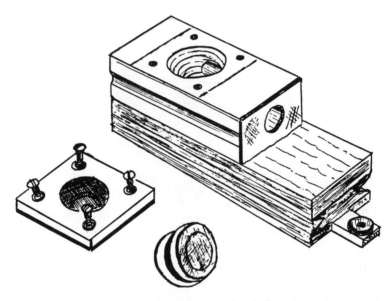

Fig. 22. A Unit Containing the Valve, Pouch, Bleed, and Pneumatic, with Valve Taken Out

If the leather valve facings have deteriorated and are rotten, this will evidence itself by the flaking off of powder from the leather when its surface is rubbed or brushed. In this case the facings must be replaced. In the case of the valves shown in Figure 20, the discs supporting the valve leather must be removed and new leather punchings inserted. In the case of the valves shown in Figure 21, the valve stem must be removed, the top and bottom valve faces cleaned with sandpaper, new leather punchings glued to the faces, and the stem replaced with a drop of glue.

When replacing the valves in the stack, care should be taken to get the seal around the valve seats completely airtight. If the valves are the type shown in Figure 20, a little shellac should be used as a seal around the lower seats. If the top seat must be removed to get to the valves, as in the case of those shown in Figure 21, the valve travel should be adjusted when the top seat is replaced. The valve clearance in most pneumatic action valves is ⅟₃₂″. Adjust the clearance, then seal the rim of the valve seat with shellac. Occasionally, the repairman will run across valves with flanged seats, made in such fashion that the clearance is automatically correct when the seat is pressed into position.

The pouches are next on the list to be considered. Here again, as with the valves, a generalization as to pouch positioning in player actions is impossible due to the variety of manufacturers' practices. However, since the repairman has already located the valves in the stack, his task is made easier in locating the pouches—as they are positioned at the lower end of the valve stems, perpendicular to them.

Many manufacturers placed their pouches in large removable boards. The board shown in Figure 23, which happens to be the board which covers the valves shown in Figure 20, is such an item. Some makers, however, constructed their pneumatic stacks in such a way that they must be split apart to reach the pouches. The pouches in the valves shown in Figure 21 are located in the lower portion of the unit blocks, which must be broken apart to reach the pouches and bleeds (see Figure 24). Most players which are constructed with the valve, pouch, and bleed in the upper part of the pneumatic itself are difficult when it comes to pouch replacement. The pneumatic must be split apart (see Figure 25), the pouches replaced, and the pneumatic must then be glued back together.

Fortunately, the pouches in many player pianos are well

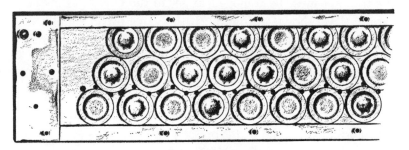

Fig. 23. A Pouch-board

preserved and not in need of replacement. Pouch leather will retain its life over long periods of time, if it is kept inside a box or other unit which prevents the circulation of atmospheric air around it. Players which have the pouches arranged in a single board, as shown in Figure 23, present no problem in checking and/or replacing pouches. The pouches should be felt with a light rotary motion of the finger, to determine whether the leather is still perfectly soft and flexible. Pouch leather which is in good condition should feel very smooth, pliable, and soft. No traces of stiffening should be evident. The repairman should inflate several of the pouches with a short length of tubing to his mouth, and should carefully watch the pouches' travel when inflated. The entire pouch should rise uniformly and smoothly, with no traces of crackling or stiffness in its motion.

Pouches which are not accessible can also be checked with a short length of tubing, through which the repairman

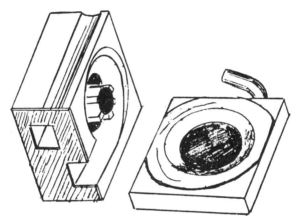

Fig. 24. A Unit-block Broken Apart to Show the Pouch. This is of the "upright" Type, with the Pouch Underneath the Valve.

can inflate the pouches. The action or unit blocks must be held such that the valves are in a vertical position, so that they can move freely. As the valves rise, carefully watch their motion. Any jerking or unevenness in their travel indicates stiff pouches. Any sort of crackling noise also spells trouble. No resistance to the rise of the valves should be noticed. The repairman should be able to hold the end of the tube several inches away from his mouth, blow on it, and watch the pouches and valves rise.

Occasionally piano manufacturers used very thin pneu-

39

matic cloth for their pouches. In most cases, this has stiffened and should be replaced.

If the repairman determines that the pouches have deteriorated and need replacing, his job is made considerably
easier if the pouches are mounted on a single board, as

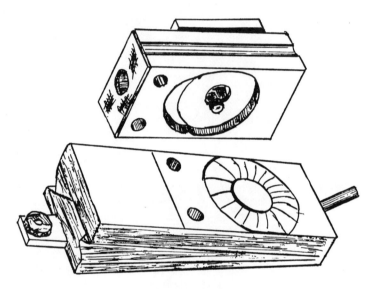

Fig. 25. The Unit Shown in Figure 22, Broken Apart to Show the Pouch

shown in Figure 23. In this case, after removing the fiber
disc in the center of some pouches, the old leather is merely
scraped off the board, which is then finish-cleaned with
sandpaper and blown off with compressed air. Care should
be taken to get all the dust and fine scraps of leather out of
the crevices. If the pouches are of the inaccessible type, the
individual blocks or other units must be broken apart using
a mallet and putty-knife. The broken halves of the units

must be kept together and not mixed up, as the two pieces must be replaced against their matching halves. Once the units have been broken apart, the leather is scraped off and the surface cleaned.

While the pouches are off the boards and the air passages are unobstructed, check the bleeds to see that they are clean. The bleeds are usually found directly beside the pouches which they vent, and they are generally small brass cup-shaped objects pressed into the wood in some manner. Occasionally bleeds were made of celluloid, and also of stiff paper—but most player piano actions contain brass bleeds. Some players have their bleeds contained in a separate chamber which is fed by suction from the supply bellows, and which can be located by tracing the tracker-bar tubing through this bleed chamber before the tubing makes its entrance into the pouch units. Run a fine wire through each bleed hole to clear dirt from it, and blow through it, preferably with compressed air. Also blow air through the holes under each pouch to remove dirt or dust which may be there.

The new pouch leather must be cut to the proper diameter. Measure the diameter of a pouch cavity, add $\frac{3}{8}''$ to it, and use this figure as the diameter of the new pouches. If the repairman has access to a lathe, an excellent pouch cutter may be made from a piece of scrap pipe of the proper diameter. Turn a sharp edge on the end of the pipe, and cut the leather with a rotary motion against end-grain wood. If no lathe is handy, the pouches can be cut by hand. In this case, a disc of the proper diameter is cut out of a piece of tin or other metal, and is used as a template around which the leather can be cut with scissors to a circular form.

41

The pouches are applied as follows: spread a thin layer of glue around the edge of each pouch cavity from its rim to about ¼″ from its edge. See that the glue is spread completely evenly and not too thickly. Take care that all glue which runs over the rim into the cavity is removed, or the motion of the pouch will be impaired. Centering the pouch over the cavity, lay it into place, smooth side up, without pressing the edges down yet.

If the repairman has a lathe, he can make a very handy tool for imparting the proper amount of "dish" to the pouches. Using wood, metal, or any material which is available, he can turn a flat-rimmed cylindrical tool with a curved bottom (see Figure 26). The depth of the curve on the bottom of the tool's face is ⅟₆₄″ less than the depth of the pouch cavity in the board. Using this tool, the proper amount of curvature may be uniformly produced in all the pouches,

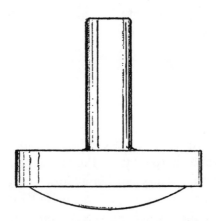

Fig. 26. Tool for Imparting the Proper "Dish" to Pouches

42

and the rims of the pouches may be pressed against the glued surface of the pouch board.

If no lathe is handy to make a tool, the pouches can be "dished" by hand. After the pouch is laid gently onto the glued surface and centered, press the *center* of the pouch down lightly until it touches the wood beneath it. Holding the center down, smooth the edges of the pouch down and press them gently against the board with a motion away

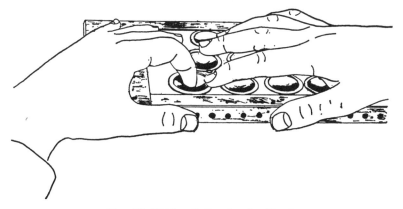

Fig. 27. "Dishing" Pouches by Hand

from the center, thus tending to draw the pouch snug (see Figure 27). See that no wrinkling or unevenness appears in the leather. If the pouch is held down in the center and the edges are smoothed down with the finger, a perfect job will result. With a little practice, the repairman will get the knack of this process. On multiple-pouch boards, the edges of adjacent pouches may overlap, but this will cause no trouble providing the overlap does not extend into the working portion of the neighboring pouches.

After the glue has dried and all the pouches are finished, replace the small fiber discs in their centers, if they were originally so equipped. Use only a tiny drop of glue in the center of the discs, as too much glue will spread onto the exposed leather surface and obstruct the motion of the pouches.

The repairman can now begin reassembling the lower portion of the pneumatic stack. Here again, description of procedure is difficult. In general, the stack should be assembled in reverse of the order in which it was taken apart. If the pouch and valve assemblies are of the unit block variety, these can be glued back together and clamped. See that their mating surfaces are entirely together, or leakage will result. New gaskets must usually be used for each unit block, as the old ones have split and torn when the blocks were broken apart. The pneumatic decks should then be assembled. Attach the rail with the push-rod guides to the top deck of pneumatics. Turn the deck upside down on the workbench. Place a little glue under each pneumatic's push-rod bracket, and insert the screws which hold it to the board. Then place the second deck on the assembly, and do the same for it. After the third deck is in place and its brackets attached, the screws, if any, holding the decks to the main supporting boards should be inserted. Then the long screws or bolts holding the ends of the stack together should be inserted. If the pouches are in board form, the board should be screwed onto the assembly. Gaskets should generally be replaced, and they can be made from white gasket leather, which is cut to size and glued to one of the mating surfaces before the joint is tightened. Some rebuilders prefer a cork composition material, available from the piano supply houses noted in a later chapter. All screws and bolts should be drawn as tightly as possible without tearing the threads out of the wood. Often, where this has happened, pieces of match-stick or toothpick can be forced into the holes, to provide material into which the screw can get a new grip. Tight joints are essential for an easy-pumping player. After the lower half of the player action stack has been reconditioned, it can be re-joined to the upper half in the same manner in which it came apart.

After the two parts of the stack have been re-united, the repairman should turn his attention to the tracker bar tubing. Many players came equipped with metallic tubing, which, in some cases, has oxidized and deteriorated with the passage of time. The repairman should pull off one or two of the metal tubes at their lower ends (if he has not already done so when separating the two parts of the stack) and blow through the tubes vigorously, from the lower end. In most cases, lead was used as the metal from which the tubing was manufactured, and this is especially prone to oxidation. If a white, dusty oxide is blown out of the tracker bar, the tubing has deteriorated on the inside and should be replaced. The lead tubing was originally slipped onto the brass nipples in the back of the tracker bar, then cemented into place. By carefully chipping away the cement, the tubing can be pulled off the tracker bar. Usually the tubing has been inserted into holes in the wood at its lower ends, from which it can be removed after the surrounding shellac or other sealer has been chipped away. If the repairman determines that the lead tubing needs to be replaced, he should remove it and replace it with rubber tubing.

REBUILDING THE PLAYER PIANO

Many pianos were originally equipped with rubber tracker bar tubing. Often this has stiffened and become rock-hard. In this case, the tubing can easily be broken off the tracker bar nipples and the nipples at its lower end, and new tubing can be installed. However, rubber can also deteriorate in such fashion that it becomes soft and sticky. In this condition it will kink easily, and will tear with slight effort, having lost all its strength. Naturally this tubing must also be replaced with new material. If the repairman finds the old tubing sticking to the tracker bar nipples, resisting all efforts to scrape it off, he should cut the old tubing at the tracker bar, remove the tracker bar from the spool box, and soak it for a few hours in gasoline. This will penetrate the old rubber and cause it to lose its grip on the nipples. After soaking, the rubber residue can be removed quickly with a stiff wire brush, which will clean the nipples and leave them ready for the new tubing after the tracker bar has dried.

In general, it can be said that almost all pianos which were originally equipped with rubber tubing should be re-tubed when they are rebuilt. Occasionally a piano will be found with tubing which, inexplicably, is still good. However, if the repairman discovers any traces of hardening, stickiness, or loss of strength, he should proceed to re-tube the piano at once. He should use the phrase "when in doubt, re-tube" as his guide if he is undecided whether to replace it or not. The low cost of tracker bar tubing and the ease with which it is replaced certainly do not warrant taking any chances by leaving old tubing in service after it has begun to deteriorate.

Some pianos were equipped with a transposer, a device which changes the key of the music being played, in case a singer wishes the music played in a certain key. This transposer is usually a lever at one side of the spool box with several notched positions, which, when moved, shifts the tracker bar from side to side, bringing different holes into alignment on the tracker bar. Pianos with transposing devices invariably have rubber tubing leading to the tracker bar. However, occasionally these pianos have rubber tubing leading only from the tracker bar to the back of the spool box, where, after passing through a row of nipples, it changes to metallic tubing. Sometimes the metal tubing in this arrangement is still good, while the rubber has hardened or otherwise deteriorated. The repairman should make it a strict point to trace the tubing carefully on pianos equipped with transposing devices, to catch any bad rubber tubing which may be in the assembly.

The actual operation of re-tubing the action is a simple one. The tubing is attached to a tracker bar nipple as it comes from the bundle. It is then run to the other nipple, and cut in such fashion that it can be attached to the nipple and still be slightly slack. The tubes are attached in order, and there is very little chance for mix-up. The sustaining pedal tube runs from the large hole at the left of the note holes, and usually goes from the tracker bar to a switch, which enables the player pianist to shut off the automatic sustaining pedal if he so desires. From the switch, it goes to the left end of the action, where it is usually attached to another nipple after the action is replaced in the piano. If the piano is equipped with an automatic tracking mechanism, this may also need to be re-tubed. Simply remove the old tubes to the automatic tracker one at a time, and replace them in this fashion.

Any other miscellaneous pneumatics around the spool box should be re-covered at this time. Pianos with pneumatic tracking devices have a pair of tracker pneumatics which must be covered. Also, some players have pneumatics which actuate friction brakes on the roll drive transmission frame, to keep proper brake tension on the roll as it rewinds and plays. These pneumatics are re-covered using exactly the same procedure as was outlined in the section on re-covering striker stack pneumatics. The only difference between stack pneumatics and any other pneumatics is one of size and shape. They are all processed using the same technique.

The air-motor should now be removed from the player action for reconditioning. This is one of the most delicate mechanisms in the piano, and it must be rebuilt skillfully and carefully for good results.

The crankshaft brackets are unscrewed from the body of the air-motor, and the entire crankshaft and sliding valve assembly can generally be lifted away from the rest of the air-motor after the connecting rods from the individual pneumatics are disconnected. The repairman must now remove the individual air-motor pneumatics from their deck, after first numbering them to prevent incorrect replacement. Air-motors were constructed in literally dozens of ways, and again the repairman must use his ingenuity in lieu of any procedure which can be given here. Sometimes the pneumatics are screwed to the deck, and sometimes they can be removed after certain metal rods which hold the assembly together have been removed. However, in many cases they have been firmly glued to the deck, and the repairman must patiently attack them with his mallet and putty-knife until

48

they have been detached. The use of a hot iron to soften the glue, as outlined in the paragraph on removal of the stack pneumatics, may come in handy here.

After the pneumatics have been detached and cleaned, they are covered with new cloth. Large air-motor pneumatics should be re-covered with air-motor cloth, which is a double-weight cloth made expressly for this purpose. Smaller air-motor pneumatics should be covered with the regular thin cloth used on the stack striker pneumatics. The only criterion for judgment in this case is whether the use of the heavier cloth will cause internal friction in the air-motor. The heavier cloth will give longer service and will be less prone to wear out at the corners. However, it will also create considerably more friction and will offer more resistance to smooth rotation of the air-motor crankshaft. Large air-motors which have plenty of power can overcome this resistance, and can safely be covered with the heavier material; but smaller ones are often not able to handle the internal friction and thus operate erratically. A good general rule for this situation is: if the perimeter of the air-motor pneumatics is twenty inches or more, use double-weight cloth. If it is under twenty inches, use thin pneumatic cloth.

When the crankshaft and connecting rods are replaced, they should be inspected for wear. The crankshaft bearings and slide valve bearings usually are equipped with felt bushings, which may be worn. If wear is evident, the bearings should be detached from the shaft and the old felt removed and replaced with new material. Powdered graphite should be worked into the new felt to provide lubrication for the bearings. The felt along the edges of the sliders should be inspected and replaced if worn. If the air-motor jerks or runs unevenly, check the sliders for warping or sticking. If any warping is detected, remove the defective slider and sand it true on a piece of fine sandpaper placed on a perfectly flat surface. After sanding, powdered graphite should be rubbed into the freshly-sanded wood to allow the slider to operate freely. If the air-motor runs unevenly and no warping of the sliders can be detected, check the adjustment of each slider to see that it is properly timed with respect to the ports which it alternately covers and uncovers. Most sliders operate over three ports, the center of which is the supply port, and the other two connect the suction supply to the pneumatics. Each slider should travel exactly the same distance each way from the center port. Check this adjustment carefully, and regulate it if necessary. Adjustment is usually made by screw threads somewhere in the slider linkage. On some air-motors, the slider rods may have to be bent to accomplish this adjustment. When the air-motor has been properly reconditioned and adjusted, it should operate without the slightest jerking or hesitation. Any irregularity in its operation evinces some defect in it which must be remedied before it is installed in the piano. Nothing is so exasperating to a player pianist as a halting, uneven motor, and the repairman should take special pains to see that the air-motor is perfect before he proceeds to the next step in the job.

At this time it is generally convenient to recondition the air-motor governor pneumatic. This is usually covered with the same material which was used on the air-motor. After the old fabric is removed from the governor, the interior parts of the unit should be thoroughly cleaned and dusted. If the piano has been used in a smoky atmosphere, the interior of the governor will sometimes be sticky and dirty. All foreign material must be removed from the moving parts. Governors which work on the knife-valve principle may need to have the surfaces of the sliding parts sanded true, then impregnated with powdered graphite. If the governor contains screens or grids, they should be cleaned well. Before applying the new pneumatic fabric, the governor should be blown out with compressed air.

After the air-motor and governor are completed, and the stack is given a final check-over (which includes oiling the roll drive transmission and checking the brake adjustments), the repairman can turn his attention to the lower bellows unit, containing the pumps and reservoir.

The first step on the lower bellows unit is to check the bellows fabric carefully, to determine whether it is in need of replacement. Many player manufacturers used good-quality bellows fabric which still retains its life. This can be quickly determined by inspecting the bellows for cracks or holes at the inner creases, and by feeling the fabric. The pump bellows should be opened to their fullest extent and the creases in their inner folds examined very carefully, as this is where the first signs of deterioration occur. Any holes or worn-through spots in the fabric spell replacement at once. Also, any crackling or hardness of the fabric means that its life has vanished and dooms it to replacement.

If no holes or worn spots are visible, and if the fabric feels as though it has retained its life, the bellows may need little attention. This is quickly determined by sealing off all external openings to the bellows, with tape or other material, and by working one or both foot pedals to build up a vacuum inside the bellows unit. A usable bellows unit should hold its vacuum for at least six or eight seconds, preferably longer. The bellows unit should be carefully checked for cracks in its wood, and if any are discovered they should be sealed by gluing a strip of pneumatic cloth over them, taking care to seal the open end-grain of the crack as well as its length. All screws in the entire unit should be tightened to insure snug, air-tight joints. If the external openings of the unit are tightly sealed off, and if the fabric is in good condition, the unit should maintain a vacuum for considerably longer than six or eight seconds. If the bellows unit meets this test, the fabric does not need to be replaced. The repairman should check the leather flap valves on the movable boards of the pumps, to determine their condition. Often they have become rotten or have curled up into an uneven strip which does not lie flat against the surface of the bellows board. In this case, they should be replaced with new strips of flap valve leather. Often the flap valves inside the pumps are in better condition than the external ones, due to their having been kept away from circulating air.

If the repairman determines that the bellows unit will maintain a strong vacuum for at least six seconds, and that its external flap valves are good (or have been replaced), he may proceed to re-install it in the piano. However, if all openings have been carefully sealed, the joints tightened, cracks sealed, and the unit will still not meet this test, it needs recovering. The bellows fabric may appear to be perfectly good, but unless the vacuum can be maintained for a minimum of six seconds, the fabric has deteriorated. Bellows fabric can be one of the most deceiving things in a player piano. The fabric can appear to be perfectly good, and can even feel soft and usable to the touch—yet it can still be porous. When the defective fabric is removed and held up to a strong light, it will be discovered to be full of thousands of tiny holes through which air can leak. The repairman can *never* take for granted that pneumatic fabric is usable simply because it looks good and feels soft. It may be as porous as a sponge. This applies to all bellows cloth, thick and thin.

If the bellows unit is in need of covering, it should be dismantled and cleaned of its old fabric. On large bellows such as pumps and reservoirs, a block plane provides the easiest method of cleaning off old fabric and glue.

Care should be taken when dismantling the reservoir, for it contains one or more powerful leaf springs which can cause serious injury. If possible, the springs should be removed through the inner opening of the reservoir before the old fabric is removed. If this is not possible, the old cloth should be partially cut away, leaving a wide strip to hold the reservoir boards from springing apart until the springs can be removed through the holes in the cloth.

While the pumps are stripped of their fabric, the inner flap valves should be checked. Unless these flaps make perfectly tight seals against their respective bellows boards, leakage will occur which will impair the performance of the piano. The flaps should be inspected for dryness or brittleness in the leather, and especially for any curling or warping. Unless the flaps lie perfectly flat against the boards, they will not be airtight. Any signs of deterioration or curling of the flaps provide immediate cause for replacement. When new flaps are installed, they should be firmly anchored at the fixed end with glue *and* tacks. If both ends are fixed, the flaps should be stretched tightly across the board before they are finally anchored. If one end of the flaps is spring-anchored, the springs should be under tension at all times, to keep the flaps tight and smooth.

When covering large spring-loaded bellows, the springs can often become troublesome. One way to get around this problem is to attach a piece of strong pneumatic cloth to the open end of the bellows. The cloth should be cut to a dimension equal to the normal span of the open end. It should be wide enough to withstand the full force of the springs, which will tend to pull it apart. The strip of cloth is attached to the open end of the pneumatic with glue and tacks. After it has thoroughly dried, the springs can be inserted into the open bellows through the sides. The bellows will then be held in an open position, and can be covered in the usual way. The fastener strip which is holding the bellows in normal position will not interfere with its operation after it is placed into service, as it can be covered up by the outer layer of cloth with no harm. Of course, the fastener strip should not be glued entirely to the outer cloth, as this would cause binding. It should be glued to the outer cloth only along the edges of the bellows, as in normal covering procedure.

The actual procedure of re-covering the bellows unit is exactly the same as that used in re-covering the strike pneumatics. The strip of heavy bellows cloth is torn or cut to a width equal to the span of the bellows, then glued on in the usual way. After drying, it is trimmed and creased. The spring blocks or any other miscellaneous hardware are then replaced on the bellows boards and the unit is reassembled.

REBUILDING

The "accessory" devices are the last individual parts of the player action to require attention. Pianos which are equipped with pneumatically-operated "soft" controls will need repair on these devices. The repairman should keep in mind that these accessory pneumatics are operated and repaired in exactly the same manner as the rest of the pneumatic system. They usually consist of a good-sized pneumatic which does the work of moving the piano action part, a valve and pouch assembly to operate the pneumatic, a suction supply tube, and a control tube leading from the control rail. The pneumatic should be re-covered, usually with air-motor cloth, and the pouch checked, the valve cleaned, and the bleed cleared as usual.

The same procedure applies to the sustaining pedal pneumatic. Occasionally manufacturers used two valves to operate the pedal pneumatic, to provide extra-quick suction flow and prompt, responsive sustaining pedal action. This pneumatic should be re-covered with the medium cloth, and the valve, pouch, and bleed assemblies checked.

The final step in the complete rebuilding of a player piano is the installation, regulation, and testing of the player action parts.

The "accessory" mechanisms should be installed first, and connected to their respective controls. The lower bellows unit may then be installed and secured in its place, and the control rods may be connected to the bellows unit at this time. The pneumatic stack should then be lifted into place and fastened. Care should be taken to see that the striking fingers on the back of the stack and the parts against which they strike are in perfect alignment. Also, there should be no lost motion between the striking fingers and the upper parts. The piano hammers should begin to move toward the strings the moment the pneumatics begin to collapse, with no lost motion or free play. Some players have an adjustment to lift the stack slightly to take up any lost motion. On pianos which have no adjustment, shims can usually be installed to move the stack slightly.

The stack supply hoses should then be connected, and the air-motor supply hose attached. New supply hose should always be used, as it is false economy to attempt to re-use the old hose. If the piano is equipped with an automatic pedal, the sustaining pedal tube should be connected at the left end of the stack. The upper and lower units should be given a general check-over to see that no rods, hoses, or other things are left disconnected.

The repairman should now test the player action for tightness and its ability to hold suction. The tracker bar should be sealed off with masking tape. The control lever should be moved to the "play" position, with the tempo lever at zero. When the pedals are pumped, the action should build up a strong vacuum inside it. After this has been built up, the repairman can determine how long this suction will maintain itself by watching the reservoir. After a good vacuum has been created and the repairman has stopped pumping the pedals, the reservoir should not reach the entirely-open point for at least five seconds.

No player action can be made entirely airtight. Every substance has a certain amount of porosity, and wood and leather are among the most porous of all materials. Every player action will gradually lose vacuum by "seepage" through the pores of the materials of which it is built. However, the natural losses of suction in a tight player action are such that it will hold a vacuum for at least five seconds, if the valves and all other external openings are tightly closed.

If the repairman determines that the action will maintain suction for approximately five seconds, he may congratulate himself on having performed a good job of rebuilding the player stack. However, if the reservoir opens in three seconds or less, the repairman should check carefully to determine whether any small leaks exist, which will rob the action of its suction.

If the repairman has a friend in the medical profession, he may be able to obtain a doctor's stethoscope, which is the finest instrument available for detecting and pinpointing vacuum leaks. A stethoscope of the open-end type is advisable, as the type with the closed diaphragm end is not satisfactory for detecting air-transmitted sounds. If a stethoscope is not readily available, a three-foot length of tracker bar tubing with one end inserted in the ear makes a usable leak detector, provided the other ear is plugged with cotton to seal out extraneous noises.

Assuming that the lower bellows unit was carefully tested before it was installed in the piano, the repairman can assume that the leak, if any, is in the upper action of the player, in the pneumatic control devices, or around the joints of the suction supply tubing. With the stethoscope or ear tube, every joint and seam in the pneumatic stack should be checked for leakage. The repairman should reach as far behind the stack as room will permit, to check the valves for hissing or leakage. The services of a second person may be put to good use while making these tests, as the repairman may find it awkward to try to pump the foot pedals, or even one pedal, while he is checking for leaks—though if necessary it can be done by one person.

If leakage is discovered around any joints or seams, the screws holding the leaking parts should be checked for tightness and if possible drawn quite tightly to eliminate the leak. If any cracks in wooden parts are discovered, they may be sealed by gluing a strip of thin pneumatic cloth over them.

If the leakage is narrowed down to one or more of the action valves, the repairman should run the test roll over the piano several times. Occasionally valves do not seat properly after they have been removed for cleaning, and often the quick repetition section of the test roll will seat the valves well. If this is not the case, and one or more of the valves still loses suction, the stack will have to be removed (if the valves are located in the rear of the stack) and the offending valve taken out, brushed, its seat checked, and re-assembled.

After the repairman has determined that the player action will maintain a vacuum for the required time, he should check the operation and repetition of each individual note, using the test roll. Every note should operate and repeat with approximately the same speed. If any note fails to operate, this means (1) that the tube leading from the tracker bar to the action may be pinched off or otherwise obstructed; (2) that the pouch for that note may have blown out or come loose from its moorings; (3) that the valve for that note is jammed or otherwise prevented from moving; (4) that the pneumatic for that note is punctured or damaged; or (5) the push-rod of the pneumatic is binding against some fixed part of the piano action. The repairman should first check for a pinched tube, and if this is found to be clear, the other things listed should be checked.

If any note makes a hissing sound while it is playing, this indicates that the valve is unable to seat itself completely against its top seat, due to dirt or some other obstruction. The valve will have to be removed and the foreign matter cleared.

If any note plays continuously and will not return to rest, this indicates (1) that the tube leading from the tracker bar is punctured or has pulled loose; (2) that the bleed is clogged, thus preventing the pouch and valve from returning to rest; (3) that the valve has somehow become jammed or stuck against its top seat and will not drop back again, or (4) that the pneumatic push-rod has jammed itself against some fixed part of the action, preventing the pneumatic from opening after its stroke. Occasionally dirt or foreign matter which is clogging a bleed can be loosened by vigorous pumping with a tracker bar pump; but if it is too firmly jammed into the bleed, the action must be dismantled to clean it out.

When all the notes are playing well, the air-motor and governor should be adjusted and calibrated. This is done using the test roll. After checking the top spool brake and adjusting it so that it maintains a moderate tension on the music roll during play, the repairman should put the test roll on the piano and begin playing it through, alternating every few seconds between very hard pumping and very light pumping. If the governor is adjusted properly, the roll will not vary in speed no matter how the piano is pumped. However, if any variation is noticed, the governor will have to be adjusted.

Governor construction varies immensely, and it is difficult

REBUILDING THE PLAYER PIANO

to give a procedure for adjusting individual units. However, governors may be generally divided into two classes:
governors with an adjusting screw which limits the collapse
of the governor pneumatic; and governors which have no
limiting screw but which have an adjustable spring tension.

If the roll speeds up when the piano is pumped hard,
screw the adjusting screw out a turn or two, if the governor
is of the limiting-screw type. If it is of the adjustable-tension
type, decrease the spring tension on the governor a little bit.

If the roll slows down or stops when the piano is pumped
hard, screw in the adjusting screw, or increase the spring
tension.

Move the adjustments only a little at a time. Never make
more than one turn of the screw or move the spring more
than one coil before trying the piano's performance again.
Four or five tries may be necessary before the air-motor runs
at a perfectly constant speed. Spend plenty of time on this
adjustment, if necessary, as it is very important.

After the governor has been properly adjusted, the tempo
of the roll should be fairly close to correct. However, it
should be exactly calibrated using the tempo-test section
of the test roll. This is a measured section which should pass
over the tracker bar in a certain time. A tempo of 70 means
that seven feet of music roll should pass the tracker bar in one
minute; likewise the number of feet at any other setting is
obtained by dividing the tempo setting by ten. If the time is
more than it should be, the roll is running too slowly; if less,
it is running too fast. Adjustment is made at the rod which
slides into the tempo box. Move the tempo lever back and
forth and watch its linkage in the lower part of the piano.
There will be leather-nut adjusters on the threaded end of

the sliding rod which enters the tempo box. To speed up the roll, the sliding rod is *usually* adjusted such that it will pull farther out of the box; however, this varies on some pianos. One trial will enable the repairman to determine which way the adjustment is made.

After a final check of the "accessories" to determine whether the automatic pedal mechanism and the expression pneumatics are operating, the repairman is ready to sample the fruits of his labor. The piano should now play well—and the repairman can discover the glow of satisfaction and pride which comes from a job well done!

THE REPRODUCING PIANO

THE REPRODUCING PIANO is a mechanical musical instrument whose function is to exactly re-create, or reproduce, the music of human pianists who recorded their playing on music rolls. It is a mechanical instrument which should sound completely non-mechanical. Ideally, the performance of a reproducing piano should give the listener the impression that the original recording artist is present, playing the piano himself. The mechanical reproducing medium should, in a sense, obliterate itself from the listener's consciousness and re-create the presence of the pianist who recorded the music roll.

Everyone is familiar with the sound of the pedal-pumped player piano which grinds out music mechanically, without variation in intensity or feeling. Contrast this with the reproducing piano, by which music is reproduced complete with every change in loudness, accent, tonal shading, nuance—in short, a living performance. The difference is akin to that of a black-and-white photograph of a vividly-colored painting, and the original painting itself. In one, the representation is monochromatic, with variations in only a single color; but in the latter, the piece takes on all its hues and colors as the artist created it. So it is with the reproducing piano, which can impart to music all the life and feeling which the composer put into it, as interpreted by some of the world's finest pianists, often the composers themselves.

The reproducing piano is basically a regular player piano with the addition of expression control mechanisms and an electric pump. It functions by varying the suction with which the pneumatics are operated, consequently varying the force with which they collapse and the intensity of the notes they play. This regulation is accomplished through some variation of the "strangling" device mentioned in the section which covers the operation of air-motor governors. The strangling mechanism varies considerably from piano to piano, but the principle is basically the same in all of them.

Three major manufacturers of reproducing pianos offered their products to the American public. These were: the American Piano Company, makers of the Ampico; the Aeolian Company, manufacturers of the Duo-Art; and the Auto-Pneumatic Action Company, makers of the Welte-Mignon "Licensee" mechanism. In 1932 the American Piano Company merged with the Aeolian Company to form the Aeolian-American Corporation (now the Aeolian Corporation, a subsidiary of Winter Piano Company) which continued the manufacture of a few Ampico and Duo-Art pianos through the 1930's and made music rolls until 1941.

THE REPRODUCING PIANO

The Ampico mechanism was available in America in the Mason & Hamlin, Chickering, Knabe, J. & C. Fischer, Marshall & Wendell, Haines Brothers, Franklin, and Ampico Symphonique pianos equipped with electric action, and in the Armstrong, Brewster, Franklin, and Foster pianos equipped with the foot-powered Marque-Ampico action. Also, the Ampico was available in leading foreign makes of pianos in all parts of the world. The Duo-Art could be purchased in the Steinway, Steck, Weber, Wheelock, Stroud, and Aeolian pianos in electric and foot-powered form. The Welte-Mignon "Licensee" action was available in one hundred and twelve different makes of American pianos, one of the finest of which was the Baldwin. The German firm of M. Welte & Sons manufactured a few pianos in this country which are known as "original" Welte-Mignons, and these came equipped with the spool box in the upper portion of the piano, rather than in the drawer as in the "Licensee" Welte actions.

Other, shorter-lived reproducing actions made their debuts on the American market, and went the way of all flesh. Some of these were; the Angelus Artrio, the Aria Divina, the Solo Carola, the Celco, the Artecho, the Apollo, and the Recordo, to name a few. The only two of these which ever caught the public fancy to any degree were the Angelus Artrio and the Recordo; and even these are so scarce today that the average player technician may never come across one. As for the others, their rarity is even greater.

The reproducing piano service information in this book is intended as supplementary information to the original service manuals, and is *not* a substitute for them. In all cases, it is quite essential that the repairman obtain a copy of the service manual for the piano on which he is working. When undertaking the complete rebuilding of a reproducing piano action, the repairman will find it helpful, sometimes quite necessary, to have a schematic tubing diagram of his piano. Reprints of the service manuals and tubing diagrams are available, as are new test rolls (see supply section). In using the service manuals and tubing schematic layouts, the repairman should not expect to find the component parts of the player action in precisely the same layout as is shown in the illustrations. All reproducing piano manufacturers changed the position and location of the parts of their actions quite often, depending upon the size of the pianos, structure of the wooden framework of grands, and other things. The repairman may have to use a little ingenuity in locating the various parts of the action.

The operation of rebuilding the reproducing piano action is scarcely different from rebuilding the 88-note player action, with the exception that the reproducing piano's expression mechanism must be repaired and the electric motor and pump serviced. However, no special techniques are required. The repairman who has successfully rebuilt several 88-note players, and has gained experience in the techniques of player piano work, can rebuild a reproducing piano action to excellent playing condition. It should be emphasized here that only the *highest* quality workmanship gives satisfactory results. The reproducing action is a delicate mechanism, and every short-cut or imperfection in the work will show up in the finished product.

Before turning the first screw to begin the repairs, the rebuilder must become totally familiar with every component part of the reproducing action. The service manual must be studied diligently and the contents thoroughly assimilated. Every detail of the operation of the action should be familiar to the repairman *before* the job is begun.

The material which follows has been divided into sections dealing with each of the three major reproducing pianos. These sections have been further divided into sub-sections dealing with testing and adjusting of the pianos using the test rolls, and general commentary in the form of "helpful hints" following the test roll information.

Before attempting to make the final adjustments and action regulations using the test roll, the repairman should see that all components of the piano are in perfect working order, *ready* to be tested.

AMPICO

To be discussed first is the Model A Ampico, built by the American Piano Company from 1916 through 1928 in grand and upright pianos. The Model A Ampico grand can easily be distinguished from its descendant, the Model B, by a glance at its roll drawer. Model A Ampico drawers were built with the tempo regulator in the form of a sliding lever in the right panel of the drawer, with the tempo scale starting at zero. This is in contrast to the Model B tempo indicator, which is in the form of a rotary pointer with calibrations starting at fifty. All Ampico uprights are Model A, as the upright was discontinued in 1929 when the Model B was first manufactured.

Before testing a Model A Ampico, the repairman should check one adjustment which is a prerequisite for satisfactory performance of all such instruments. The relative positions of the moving parts of the expression mechanisms must be precisely established. Specifically, the positions of lever arm number 5, regulator valve stem number 21, regulator valve number 20, stop collar number 22, and spring pneumatic number 23 (referring to Illustration 3A, page 8, 1923 Ampico Inspector's Reference Manual) must be adjusted. In upright pianos this is easily done without removing the expression mechanisms. In grands, it is occasionally necessary to remove the mechanisms in order to get a clear view of lever arm number 5. This adjustment is as follows: loosen the upper pair of leather nuts number 8 in the illustration, so that lever arm number 5 is free to move on rod number

21. Press downward on rod number 21 (or pull downward on spring pneumatic number 23) so that regulator valve number 20 is pressed against its seat. Holding the rod in this position, tighten upper leather nuts number 8 so that lever arm number 5 is perfectly parallel to the lower board on which the three intensity pneumatics are mounted. Then, still pressing the rod downward, keeping valve number 20 against its seat, adjust stop collar number 22 so that there is approximately $\frac{3}{16}''$ clearance between the collar and the guide bushing number 10. Finally, still pressing the rod downward, loosen the lower leather nuts number 8 and adjust the spring pneumatic so that the clearance between the inner edges of the pneumatic's boards at the open end is $\frac{7}{8}''$. Take note that this is *not* the dimension across the entire open end of the pneumatic, but only the distance across the "working area" of the cloth. The parts of the expression mechanisms will now be in their proper relationship.

While checking the adjustment of the moving parts of the expression mechanism, the repairman should see that the assembly consisting of spring pneumatic number 23, rod number 21, and lever arm number 5 is perfectly free to move without the slightest friction. Occasionally, due to shrinking or swelling of lever arm 5, the rod 21 will have become slightly bound in its bushings. The operation of the entire expression mechanism is dependent upon the ability of this assembly to move instantaneously, and no pains should be spared to see that it is free. If the three intensity pneumatics attached to lever arm 5 have not been re-covered, they should be carefully checked, and they must be perfectly soft and pliable. If this is not the case, they should be re-covered at once. The leather nuts which attach the rod 21 to the spring pneumatic 23 and lever arm 5 must not be too tight, as this can bind the moving parts. After determining that the entire assembly moves perfectly freely, a tiny quantity of light, non-gumming oil can be placed on the rod and worked into the top and bottom bushings to insure frictionless operation.

The repairman should remember that the Model A Ampico striker pneumatic stack is a double-valve action (see Chapter I). The expression and control valves in the Model A are single-valve, however.

The following instructions apply only to the new Ampico test rolls which are furnished by Player Piano Company and the piano supply houses (see supply section). For reasons of economy, the Model A and Model B test rolls have been combined into one large roll which will test both pianos. This combined test roll is different from the original test rolls, and the information which follows applies only to the combined rolls.

To test the Model A Ampico, proceed as follows: place the test roll on the piano, and turn on the motor. Set the tempo at zero. Listen for noises in the pump, belt, and motor, and eliminate any which are present. Listen for leakage around joints and at hose connections.

Test 1, tempo test. Set the tempo lever at eighty. The roll should travel from the first chord to the last chord in one minute. If adjustment is necessary, vary the setting of the nuts on the steel wire which acts on the governor spring (see Figure G, Illustration 7, page 14, manual). On grands the governor is located at the extreme rear of the right compartment in the drawer. On uprights its location may be

THE REPRODUCING PIANO

seen in the Rear Assembly illustration on page 4 of the manual.

Test 2, slow crescendo test. With the roll running at tempo forty, the crescendo pneumatics should slowly close as the holes come over the tracker bar. They should be approximately closed when the second chord strikes, and approximately open when the third chord strikes. This differs slightly from piano to piano, and if a small discrepancy is noted, it is no cause for worry. On most Model A Ampicos, no adjustment is available with which to vary the speed of the crescendo anyway. However, some early Ampicos have adjusting screws on the side of each crescendo pneumatic, with which the speed can be regulated.

Test 3, fast crescendo test. With the roll running at tempo forty, the crescendo pneumatics should close quickly when holes number 2 and 5 are opened by the roll. The same procedure applies as in test 2.

Tests 4 through 9 apply to the Model B Ampico only, and should be disregarded when testing the Model A.

Test 10 is a minimum intensity test. With the roll stopped and the cancel holes opened by the appropriate perforations, remove one of the treble tubes leading to the tracker bar and attach a vacuum gauge to it. With the modifying switch in the "Brilliant" position, the gauge should read approximately seven inches of water. If adjustment is necessary, vary the setting of the screw-adjusted spring on the treble crescendo pneumatic (see Illustration 2, page 6, manual). To increase the gauge reading, increase tension on the spring; to decrease reading, decrease tension. Then, do the same to the bass side of the mechanism. This will provide

REBUILDING THE PLAYER PIANO

the basic adjustment of the minimum playing level, a very important setting.

Test 11 applies to the Model B Ampico only.

Test 12 is a re-check of the minimum intensity adjustment made in test 10.

Test 13 checks the action of the intensity valves operated by tracker bar holes number two on each end of the bar. Attach the gauge to bass and treble tracker bar tubes successively and note its action when the number two holes are opened. There should be a very slight increase in the gauge reading when the holes open. If not, check the operation of the number two intensity valves. The gauge should return to the minimum setting when the number two holes are closed off by the roll. If this does not occur, check the operation of the bass and treble cancel valves.

Test 14 checks the action of the number four holes. Proceed exactly as in test 13. The increase in the gauge reading should be slightly more than in test 13.

Test 15 checks the action of the number six holes. Proceed as in the above two tests, noting a still higher increase in reading.

Test 16 applies to the Model B Ampico only.

Test 17 is another check of the minimum intensity level.

Tests 18 through 24 are checks of the operation of the expression locks and cancels. Before making these tests, it may be wise to re-read page 9 of the service manual in order to refresh the memory as to the operation of these locks and cancels. Attach the gauge to the bass and treble tracker tubes successively, and run the test roll such that the tests follow each other. With each test, a higher gauge reading should be noted, and this should be followed by a brief

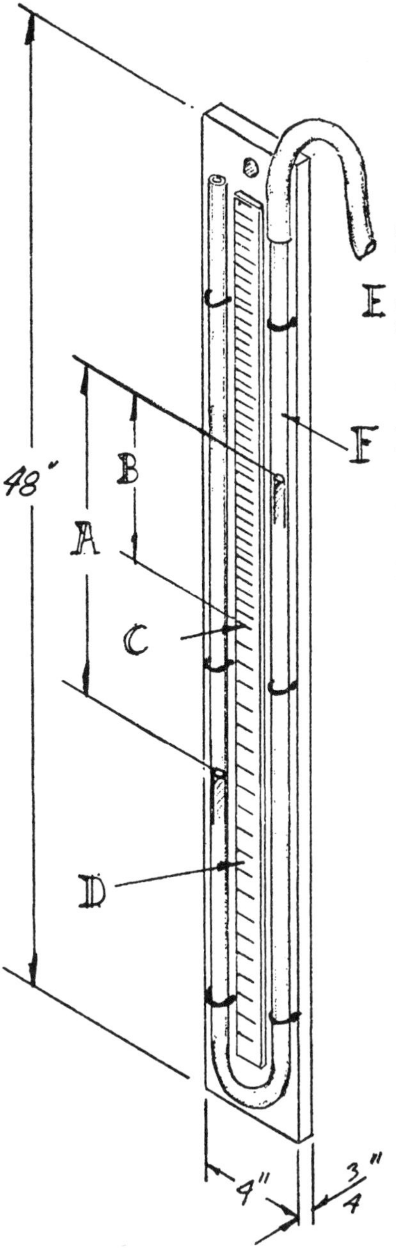

HOME-MADE VACUUM GAUGE

If the repairman does not wish to invest in a dial-type gauge such as can be secured from the piano supply houses, a simple gauge of this type can be made quickly and easily. One or the other type is a necessity for proper regulation of reproducing pianos.

F is either clear plastic or glass tubing, with an inside diameter of at least ¼ inch. It is formed to a U-shape and fastened to the board by any convenient means; if glass is used a rubber tube can be used to form the U at the bottom. D is a yardstick or other scale marked off in inches. One end of the tubing is left open to the atmosphere, and the other is connected to a piece of rubber tubing, as at E, which is used to connect to the vacuum source being tested.

The tubing is filled to its midpoint C with water. If it is colored with ordinary vegetable coloring matter, found in most household kitchens, it is easier to read.

When a vacuum is introduced at E, the water will rise in that side of the tube, and the total amount of vacuum is indicated by the number of inches between the tops of the water columns, as A. This will be the difference between the numbers of inches on the scale D.

A direct-reading gauge can be made by marking a scale with half-inches indicated as inches, and making sure that the 0 inch mark always coincides with the level of the water at rest, either by making the scale adjustable, or by making sure the amount of water is such that it always comes to the 0 point at rest. Such an arrangement is easier to work with, as the readings can always be made directly such as at B.

Fig. 28

return to the minimum intensity level before the next expression lock occurs. Any failure to lock or cancel can be traced either to inoperative valves in the expression blocks or to a blocked tube from the tracker bar to the expression mechanism.

Test 25 checks individual notes. With the tempo at seventy, listen as each note strikes. Any failure of a note to speak is due to a pinched tube, a defective valve, or some mechanical jamming in the action. The notes should speak softly, but none should miss. If any notes do not quite speak, remove and examine their valve blocks, cleaning the leather facings of the valves and checking them for grains of dirt which would prevent the valves from seating properly. After this is done, it is a good idea to repeat test 25 under full power, to check for leaking valves. With the stack housing cover removed, pull off the number two tubes leading to both crescendo mechanisms, and run the test roll through test 25. The notes will play at full volume, and any leaking valves will be indicated by a hissing noise. The leaks, of course, must be corrected. Replace the crescendo tubes after the test is completed.

Test 26 is a visual test to check whether the soft pedal action (hammer rail lift) is operating. Adjust the hammer rail so that the hammers are approximately one inch from the strings when the soft pedal is on. In Ampico grands, the soft pedal pneumatic is usually located on the front wall of the large rear compartment, although sometimes it is built into the upper part of the pedal lyre. In uprights its location is shown on page 2 of the manual. Adjustment is made by varying the setting of the large screw in the pneumatic.

Test 27 is a listening test to check the hammer rail travel

and to confirm the adjustment made in test 26. The chord struck at the third intensity with the pedal on should sound with the same loudness as the chord struck at the first intensity with the pedal off.

Test 28 checks the travel and action of the sustaining pedal. Adjust the pedal so that the dampers are lifted about ⅛″ from the strings. In most Ampico grands, the sustaining pedal pneumatic is located behind the piano action, which must be removed to gain access to it. Some grands locate it near the soft pedal pneumatic in the rear compartment of the piano, while others have it directly at the top of the pedal lyre with the soft pedal pneumatic. In uprights, its location is usually as shown on page 4 of the manual, but may vary from piano to piano. After making this test, run the test through again at tempo seventy. The chord struck with the dampers lifted should not sound through the second perforation. If this occurs, the pedal action is sluggish and must be quickened. Check the linkage for lost motion, and check the sustaining pedal valve for proper operation. Dirt in the sustaining pedal valve bleed is a common cause of slow pedal return. See that the pedal pneumatic supply tube is not pinched or blocked.

Test 29 applies to a small percentage of Model A Ampicos. It checks the action of the sustaining pedal compensator, which was only built into Model A Ampicos in 1927 and 1928. The sustaining pedal compensator in the Model A action takes the form of two very small square pneumatics which are mounted on top of the bass and treble spring pneumatics (number 23, Illustration 3A, page 8, 1923 manual). These two small pneumatics are connected to steel rods, which run downward and are connected to the lower decks of the spring pneumatics. A quick glance will tell whether these two small pneumatics are present on the piano being serviced, and if they are not, then the piano has no pedal compensator and test 29 should be skipped. However, if they are present, their action should be checked. They are actuated directly from the sustaining pedal valve, and their function is to make the piano play very slightly softer when the sustaining pedal is on. The engineers at the Ampico laboratories discovered that a slightly greater volume of sound comes from the striking of any given notes when the pedal is on than when it is off. To allow for this, they added the pedal compensator, which will slightly reduce the volume of the piano when the pedal is on. To check the action of the two small pneumatics, simply remove their tubes and see that they get suction when the pedal is on. The rod should be adjusted so that the pneumatics are approximately halfway open in their rest position.

Test 30 is a maximum playing capacity test, which will show whether the piano is capable of playing large, crashing chords at high volume, and large numbers of notes in rapid succession. A perfectly-operating Ampico should play through this test without showing signs of insufficient vacuum or dropping off in volume.

Check the rewind performance of the piano by watching the rewind perforation cross the tracker bar. The shift to rewind should be positive and smooth. The governor should by-pass itself and the air-motor should run at full speed during rewind. Turn the repeat switch to "on" and watch the action of the repeat mechanism as the roll reaches the end of the rewind cycle. If the rewind or repeat systems are operating incorrectly, the reader is referred to Illustration 7 on page 14 of the 1923 manual for the schematic layout of the systems. On many Ampico grands and some uprights, the trigger which operates the electric motor shutoff and the repeat mechanism takes the form of a small hole drilled in the take-up spool on its left side, rather than the so-called "spoon valve" illustrated as number 19 in Illustration 7. Ampicos with these drilled take-up spools should always be lubricated at the take-up spool bearings. The spool should be removed, and the ball bearing at its left end should be taken out and lubricated with heavy oil. The leather washers under the bearing should be removed and coated with Vaseline or grease to insure an air-tight seal which will prevent leakage and thus prevent the piano from turning itself off during play. The rewind-repeat-shutoff system of the Model A Ampico is a rather complex mechanism, and a thorough understanding of all parts of Illustration 7 is necessary to service it.

The amplifier should now be tested. Read page 18 of the manual for a diagram and explanation of this mechanism, and also see Illustration 9, page 16, for the location of the amplifier. With the wooden cover of the amplifier pneumatic removed and the modifying switch at "Medium," turn the piano on with a blank space of paper on the tracker bar and the tempo at zero. Connect the vacuum gauge to one of the tracker bar tubes, bass or treble. Pull off the number 2 tubes to the crescendo pneumatics so that they collapse completely. With the modifier at "Medium," the gauge should rise to 20″ but no higher. If adjustment is necessary, rotate spring number 7 in Illustration 9, page 16. Tighten the spring to increase the reading, loosen it to decrease it. Then, turn the modifying switch to "Brilliant," with the crescendo tubes still removed. The vacuum gauge should rise to between 30″ and 35″ as the amplifier pneumatic closes. If adjustment is necessary, turn screw number 8 in Illustration 9. The "Subdued" position should now be adjusted, and this position requires separate adjustment for the bass and treble parts of the action. Turn the switch to "Subdued," at which time the gauge should fall to about 12″. Adjustment is made by turning leather nuts number 17 in Illustration 3A, page 8, 1923 manual, on the re-regulator pneumatics' stems. When this is completed, make a final check of the trigger action of the amplifier control box (see page 18, manual) by replacing the crescendo tubes, turning the modifying switch to "Brilliant," and again pulling off the crescendo tube on the side to which the gauge is attached. Watch the gauge and the amplifier pneumatic: as the gauge reaches approximately 15″, the pneumatic should close. Consult page 18 of the manual for details.

The following section is composed of random comments concerning the repair and service of the Model A Ampico. The information presented is derived solely from the writer's personal experience with the Ampico and its service problems.

By this time, many of the original castings in the drawer or spool box of Model A Ampicos have deteriorated and must be repaired or replaced. Many of them were cast of so-called "pot metal" or "white metal" which tends to swell and warp over the years. Especially prone to this deterioration are the row of rotary switches on the left side of the Ampico spool box, and the roll drive transmission frame on the right of the spool box. In some Ampicos the deterioration has progressed to such an extent that these parts have turned into a corroded lump of oxide. However, if only minor warping and "growing" has occurred, the repairman can re-use the old switches and transmission frame after some restorative treatment. The entire row of switches can be removed, after their tubing has been detached, and the individual switches removed from their mounting board (speaking of the grand) and taken apart. Only one switch should be processed at a time, as they are easily mixed up, and no two are alike. The mating surfaces of the switches can be restored to a smooth, tight fit by rubbing them over a piece of medium sandpaper on a perfectly flat surface, and then finishing them up with fine sandpaper. A light coat of grease on the mating surfaces will act as a seal to prevent leakage. All dust should be blown out of the switches before assembly. If any serious cracks on the outer surfaces of the switches admit air leakage, these can be filled with glue and allowed to dry. Each switch should be checked with a tube to see that it is perfectly tight before installation.

The roll drive transmission frame should also be checked for this same "growing" of the metal of which it is cast. With the shifting control lever halfway between the play and re-wind positions, spin the gears by hand and observe their motion, noting that they are free in their bearings and that the shifter mechanism works as it should. If the bearings are frozen or the shafts rotate unevenly, the transmission frame must be removed and the bearings freed. A good way to do this is to clamp the frame in a vise (gently, so as not to crack it) and feed a mixture of oil and powdered pumice stone into the lubrication holes in the frame while spinning the shafts with a hand drill. Machinists' cutting oil is best for this purpose, but if this is not available regular penetrating oil can be used, or even thin motor oil if nothing else is at hand. The oil will carry the pumice into the bearings, where it will gradually wear away the distorted metal until the shafts spin freely again. The pumice must be flushed out of the bearings with gasoline or thin motor oil, and the bearings should be lubricated with medium oil before use. Also, attention must be given to the face of the sliding valve port in the transmission frame. Like the rotary switches, this is often warped or cracked, and if this has occurred the face must be smoothed with sandpaper as in the case of the switches. The face should be coated with a thin layer of grease before use.

Occasionally an Ampico will be found in which the rotary switches and the transmission frame have deteriorated to the point at which they can no longer be restored. In this case, new ones can be purchased from Player Piano Company (see the chapter on supplies).

The air-motor governor of the Model A Ampico contains a mesh screen which is prone to clog with dust and dirt and thus restrict the operation of the air-motor. When re-covering the governor, this screen should always be cleaned. In some cases, the screen will have become so clogged that the roll will not travel at normal tempos. In this case, the screen must be cleaned, and since there is no outside access to it, the governor fabric will have to be removed and the governor re-covered after the screen is cleaned.

Very close to the end of production of the Model A Ampico, a few pianos were produced with amplifiers which were different from the regular Model A amplifier. These use a sleeve pneumatic which operates a curtain valve, much in the manner of the Model B Ampico amplifier mechanism. This sleeve pneumatic operates just like the regular pneumatic in other Model A amplifiers, and its adjustments are obvious upon inspection.

Ampicos must be checked for corrosion of the metal elbows in the large vacuum lines which supply the pneumatic stack. Often these have oxidized to the point at which their walls are too thin to withstand use or have been partially eaten away. Elbows which have deteriorated to this point can be replaced with copper pipe elbows of the proper diameter, which are available at any hardware store. If the elbows have begun to oxidize but have not reached the point at which they are no longer fit for use, the oxidation can be halted by cleaning the inner and outer surfaces of the elbows as well as possible, then dipping them in shellac, which will seal their surfaces and prevent further oxidation.

If the supply line elbows have oxidized, the repairman must make it a point to clean the interior channels of the pump, as the oxide flakes will have been drawn into the pump, clogging the screens and preventing tight closing of the flap valves. The pump must be removed from the piano and taken apart on the bench. Both the steel face plate containing the drive wheel and the opposite wooden plate must be removed to do the job properly. The wooden panels on the outer surfaces of the pump must be removed, and the channels thoroughly cleaned. The surfaces of the flap valves in the interior of the individual bellows should be cleaned as well as possible. This is a ticklish job, but a vital step in restoring the pump to peak performance. With a screwdriver or other long tool, the flap can be pressed inward gently, while the dirt imbedded in it can be picked off with a fine pair of tweezers. A small, stiff brush should be used to give the flap a final brushing-up after the dirt has been removed from it. An amazing amount of dirt can become lodged in these flap valves, and the repairman should spare no effort to remove all of it. A strong light is an asset in doing this job.

Before re-assembling the pump, lubricate the center spindle bearings with heavy oil. The cap on the interior bearings can be removed and the oil fed into the double ball bearings. The bearings in the steel face plate of the pump have no access, and the oil must be injected into the bearings around the retainer ring and allowed to penetrate before the pump is re-installed.

Probably one of the least-serviced parts in any reproducing piano is the electric motor. This should be removed from the piano, completely dismantled, cleaned, and thoroughly lubricated before the piano is put back into service. Motors in grand pianos hang with their shafts in a vertical position, and this throws the weight of the armature shaft onto a thrust washer at the lower end of the armature. These thrust washers are subjected to conditions of intense heat and friction, and they must *always* be lubricated properly. The motor must be taken apart to get to the thrust washer, which is usually a compound washer composed of numerous thin washers of brass or steel. Medium engine oil should be used to lubricate this washer, and light engine oil should be injected into the cotton packing at each end of the shaft to provide lubrication for the bearings. Upright pianos have their motors mounted horizontally, which eliminates the problem of the thrust washer, and these can be lubricated by injecting oil into the cotton packing without removing the motor from the piano. However, grands must be treated differently, and their motors should be removed at least once a year and taken apart for servicing.

Many Model A Ampico pumps were built with wooden connecting rods running from the crankshaft to the individual pump bellows. These wooden rods have spring-loaded wedges of wood in their centers, which are supposed to keep the connecting rod bearings tight and prevent noise. In some pumps, disagreeable knocking noises occur when the pumps are running, due to wear or other looseness at these bearings. In most cases, this knocking can be remedied by removing the small coil springs which keep the wedge-shaped pieces of wood pressed into the connecting rods, and then replacing them with stiffer springs. Before this is done, however, the knocking rods should be removed and checked for wear on the felt bushings which line their holes. If the felt is badly worn, it should be replaced before re-installing the rods and inserting stiffer springs in the wedges.

A provocative source of trouble in the Model A Ampico is the so-called "cancel pneumatic" on the automatic expression cutout block (see number 16, Illustration 4, page 10, 1923 manual). Invariably, the cloth pad on the arm of the cancel pneumatic has become stiff or otherwise deteriorated so that it fails to seal off the two protruding tubes, 7B and 7T. This arm should always be re-faced with a strip of gasket leather, and the repairman should check very carefully to see that the two tubes are tightly sealed when the pneumatic is collapsed. Any leakage at these tubes will prevent the expression locks from working, and the performance of the piano will be completely unsatisfactory.

The leather on the brass pads of the two tracker "ears"

should be checked, and almost inevitably replaced. Even though the tracker mechanism may work, in all but the most unusual cases this leather has deteriorated and is no longer useful. On many upright Ampicos this task is quite simple, as the pads are exposed at the rear of the upper roll compartment and may quickly be removed and replaced. However, most Ampicos have the tracker ears protruding directly through the tracker bar; and in this case access to them must be gained by removing one of the thin boards which run directly downward, or backward, from the tracker bar. In the case of the grand, this is done by removing the long bottom strip underneath the drawer, then sliding the thin board directly downward from the tracker bar. The board is mounted in small tracks, and will drop out of the bottom of the drawer without trouble. In uprights, the construction varies from piano to piano, but in most cases the top board leading back from the tracker bar may be removed by taking out several small screws in its surface.

In rare cases, the metal tubing which leads from the tracker bar of an Ampico may have deteriorated, and must be replaced. In the case of the grand, space is a problem. However, the tubing can successfully be replaced with rubber tubing, providing care is used. The brownish cement which holds the lead tubing onto the brass nipples must be chipped away, the lead tubing pulled off, the nipples cleaned of all fragments of cement and lead, and the new tubing installed.

Some Model A Actions were made with the so-called lost motion pneumatics, as found on the Model B. These pianos were built toward the end of the Model A's production, after the Model B had been conceived. They date from 1927 and

1928. The lost motion pneumatics (see Figure 16 opposite Figure 14, and also text covering soft pedal valve, in the 1929 service manual) are constructed approximately identically with those of the Model B Ampico. In the few uprights which were built with a lost motion device, it takes the form of a large pneumatic under the back of the key-bed which pushes two rods against brackets on the striker rail of the player action.

Some collectors who own other player pianos may decide to convert their Ampicos such that they will play Ampico rolls only. Although a properly-rebuilt Ampico should give its owner no trouble from the 88-note mechanism, it is an undeniable fact that the fewer the operating parts, the fewer the leaks and chances for trouble to occur. The Model A Ampico can be converted to play exclusively from Ampico rolls in a very short time, and this can be done without making the slightest physical alteration in the construction of the mechanism. The first step is to by-pass the automatic expression cutout block (see page 10, manual) so that the expression tubing coming from the tracker bar runs directly to the expression mechanism, without passing through the cutout block. This is done by simply removing the tubes, and joining the matching pairs with brass nipples. However, the suction supply to the expression cutout block should not be shut off, as a tube leads from the cancel pneumatic to the rewind cutout block (Figure H in Illustration 7, page 14, manual), and if vacuum were not present in this tube, the piano would not rewind automatically. An alternative is to tee tube 17 (Illustration 7) into the tube just to its left which operates pouch 29, so that when pouch 29 is drawn away from its seat, pouch 30 follows it: then the suction supply to the expression cutout block can be shut off. Also, the "Pedal" switch in the spool box can be by-passed by connecting its two tubes with a nipple. Finally, the tubes leading from the finger buttons to connections number 44 on the bass and treble expression units (see Illustration 3B, page 8, manual) should be disconnected and tied off such that no air can get through them. The piano will now play Ampico rolls exclusively, and its originality has not been disturbed, as it can be re-converted to play 88-note rolls in just a few minutes.

The Model B Ampico was built from 1929 until approximately 1940. In its latter years it was built only on special order—hence the extreme rarity of the later specimens. The Model B Ampico represented a complete re-engineering of the Model A. Only the basic concept of an intensity system coupled with a crescendo system remained the same. By the most unfortunate of coincidences, the introduction of the Model B Ampico came shortly before the paralyzing stock-market crash of 1929, and it was destined to be marketed throughout its life span during years when most of the American public had very few dollars to spend on luxuries such as reproducing pianos. Had the Model B Ampico been produced five years earlier, during the zenith of the reproducing piano's popularity, many more of these superb instruments would be extant. Model B Ampicos are rare today, and the remaining examples are highly prized by collectors.

Before testing the Model B Ampico mechanism, the same advice applies as it did to the Model A, and indeed as it does to every player: make absolutely certain that the player mechanism is tight, well-lubricated, and in condition to warrant testing it. Keep in mind that the Model B action is single-valve, unlike its Model A ancestor.

Instructions refer to the test roll furnished by Player Piano Company or the other piano supply houses, which will test both the Model A and Model B Ampicos.

Place the test roll on the piano, and turn on the motor. Set the tempo to the off position. Listen for noises in the pump, belt, and motor, and for leakage around joints and at hose connections. Eliminate any undue noise or leakage before proceeding.

Test 1, tempo test. Set the tempo indicator at eighty. The roll should travel from the first chord to the last chord in one minute. If adjustment is necessary, vary the setting of nut F in Figure 21 of the 1929 Ampico service manual. If the roll travels too fast, turn the nut F so as to relieve some of the tension on spring I, and vice versa. While making this adjustment, it is always wise to lubricate the bearings of the drawer motor and the shafts. Use very light oil and inject only five or six drops into the felt packing at the motor bearings, and less at friction points of the shafts. Use *only* graphite grease to lubricate the contact area of the governor arms (point D in Figure 21). Use a little graphite grease on the worm gears, but not enough to smear—just enough to give a thin coating to the gears. See that the governor weights are free to move easily; if not, place a very tiny drop of oil at point C in Figure 21 and work the weight assemblies back and forth until they move freely.

Tests 2 and 3, crescendo tests. No adjustment to vary the speed of the crescendo or diminuendo is available on the Model B Ampico, so use these tests only to determine whether the slow and fast crescendo and diminuendo are operating.

Test 4, first amplification. The Model B Ampico contains an amplifier which is totally different from the Model A. This amplifier is very thoroughly illustrated and explained in the 1929 service manual, to which the reader is referred. The Model B amplifier makes use of an additional hole in the tracker bar, called the OB hole (the "zero-B" hole), which is controlled by corresponding perforations in Ampico rolls cut after 1927. This OB perforation is used in tests 4 through 9 of the test roll. To make test 4, connect the vacuum gauge to the "Pump" test outlet under the center of the piano. With the roll running at tempo seventy, the gauge should rise to between 21″ and 29″ when the OB perforation passes over the tracker bar. If this (or any of the tests from 4 through 9) does not work, check the amplifier mechanism for worn parts or other trouble. Occasionally the lugs N and O on rod M (Figure 9, 1929 manual) are worn, and a new connecting rod must be made before the amplifier will function properly. Often the spring which opens the amplifier trigger pneumatic must be removed and strengthened by bending it open.

Test 5, second amplification. With the roll running, the gauge should rise to between 30″ and 40″ when the OB perforation crosses the tracker bar. *Caution:* be sure to run through tests 4 and 5 without interruption, as rewinding the roll between the two tests will throw the amplifier back to normal and will cause it to rise only to first amplification on test 5. Tests 4 through 9 must be made in this fashion, without rewinding the roll between any of them.

Test 6, cancel to first amplification. When perforation OB

crosses the tracker bar, the gauge should return to between 21″ and 29″.

Test 7, cancel to normal. When perforation OB crosses the tracker bar, the gauge should return to between 15″ and 21″.

Test 8, normal to second amplification. The gauge should rise in two steps to between 30″ and 40″.

Test 9, cancel to normal. The gauge should return quickly to between 15″ and 21″.

Test 10 is a minimum intensity test. Connect the gauge to the "Treble" outlet under the piano. With the roll motion stopped and with the cancel holes opened by the perfora- tions, the gauge should read 6″ when the first intensity ad- juster (Figure 5, manual) is set at its approximate middle notch. If adjustment is necessary, regulate screw E in Figure 4, manual. This usually appears as a small screw with a knurled lock ring which must be adjusted through a hole in the wooden cover which houses the pneumatic stack on the bottom of the piano. Make this test separately for the bass and treble, attaching the gauge to the two outlets suc- cessively and regulating each side individually.

Test 11, sub intensity test. The Model B Ampico incor- porates an additional step whereby its playing may be ren- dered a shade softer than that of the Model A. This is controlled by the extreme treble hole on the tracker bar, known as the OT hole (the "zero-T" hole). This perforation in the rolls is also known as the "sub" perforation, because it operates the sub-intensity mechanism. Its operation is fully explained by Figure 8 of the manual and the accompanying text. To make test 11, connect the gauge to the treble test outlet and run the roll. When the OT perforation crosses the tracker bar, the gauge should drop to between 5″ and 5½″. repeat this test with the gauge connected to the bass test outlet.

Test 12, another check of the zero intensity level.

Test 13 checks the action of the intensity valves operated by holes number two on each end of the tracker bar. (*Note:* it must be remembered that holes number two on the Model B Ampico are actually the *third* holes from the ends of the tracker bar, due to the addition of the OB and OT holes. This applies to all expression holes on the Model B.) Attach the gauge to the bass and treble test outlets successively and note its action when the number two holes are opened. There should be a slight increase in the reading with the holes opened. If not, check the operation of the intensity valves.

Test 14 checks the action of the number four holes. Proceed exactly as in test 13. The gauge rise should be slightly more than in test 13.

Test 15 checks the action of the number six holes. Proceed as in tests 13 and 14, noting a still higher increase in gauge reading.

Tests 16 through 24 are tests of the expression locks and cancels. This operation is well explained in Figures 6 and 7 of the 1929 manual and in the accompanying text. If difficulty is noted with the tests, or if any of the valves will not lock or cancel, the trouble may be remedied by referring to these illustrations, and the text, and by making appropriate repairs. These locks and cancels are vital to the operation of the piano, and care should be taken to see that they work perfectly. The tests must be performed successively on the bass and treble sides.

THE REPRODUCING PIANO

Test 25 checks the individual notes. With the tempo set at seventy, listen as each note strikes. Any failure of a note to speak is due to a defective pneumatic, a troublesome valve block, mechanical jamming in the action, or a stopped tube. The notes should speak softly, but none should miss. If irregularity in the notes is noticed, the Ampico Note Compensation test roll should be used (available from Player Piano Company or the other supply houses). This is a test roll which enables the repairman to adjust the volume of the individual notes by varying the opening of the striker pneumatics (this cannot be adjusted on the Model A Ampico). This is an *important* test, as the performance of the piano at low volume level is quite dependent upon the regularity of adjustment of the pneumatics with the Note Compensation roll. After running test 25 at low volume level, it is a good idea to pull off the tubes leading to the intensity valves and run the test again at full volume. Listen with the ear close to the individual note valves, and any leaking valves will be indicated by a hissing noise. Replace the intensity tubes after the test is completed.

Test 26 checks the operation of the soft pedal (hammer rail lift). The hammers should move to approximately ⅞″ from the strings with the soft pedal on. This can be adjusted by varying the setting of the screw in the movable board of the soft pedal pneumatic, located at the front of the large compartment under the back of the piano. While making this test, it is wise to check the operation of the lost motion pneumatics (see Figure 16, manual, and text opposite Figure 14).

Test 27 is a listening test to check the hammer rail travel and to confirm the adjustment made in test 26. The chord struck at the third intensity with the soft pedal on should sound with the same loudness as the chord struck at the first intensity with the pedal off.

Test 28 checks the action of the sustaining pedal (damper lift). The pedal should lift the dampers approximately ⅛″ away from the strings. Check to see that the damper action is uniform from bass to treble. Adjustment of the lift is made by varying the position of the screw in the sustaining pedal pneumatic, which in most cases is located behind the piano action. After checking the pedal action, run the test through at tempo seventy. The chord struck with the dampers raised should not sound through the second pedal perforation. If this occurs, the pedal return is sluggish and must be quickened up. Check the linkage for lost motion and sticky action, and check the sustaining pedal valve for proper operation. Dirt in the pedal valve bleed is a common cause of slow pedal return.

Test 29 checks the sustaining pedal compensator. The operation of this mechanism is fully explained in the text beneath Figure 14 of the manual. No adjustment is recommended for this mechanism unless absolutely necessary, in which case it is done by regulating screws L and M of the first intensity adjuster (Figure 5, manual). Model B pianos which are equipped with a subduing switch in the drawer have no adjustment on the sustaining pedal compensator mechanism.

Test 30 is a maximum playing capacity test, which shows whether the piano is capable of playing large, crashing chords at full volume. A properly-operating Ampico should play through this test with ease.

Watch the rewind perforation as it crosses the tracker

bar. There should be a smooth, positive shift from play to rewind—no jerking or hesitation should be apparent. The rewind speed of the Model B Ampico can be varied by adjusting screw H of Figure 21 in the 1929 manual.

Check the repeat mechanism by turning the drawer switch to the repeat position. When about fifteen turns of paper are left on the takeup spool, the rewind will slow down, and the transmission will be shifted to the play position when the last turn of paper begins to unroll from the take-up spool. The operation of the rewind-repeat system is covered very adequately in the 1929 service manual.

Put the roll back on the take-up spool and run it until the stack turns on. Then, stop the roll, but leave the motor running. The operation of the pedal regulator should now be checked (see Figure 13, manual). Attach the gauge to the "Pedal" test outlet under the piano and adjust the spring on the pedal regulator so that the gauge reading is one or two inches lower than normal pump suction (as determined from the "Pump" test outlet). The function of the pedal regulator is described in the manual under Figure 13. The leather on the sleeve pneumatic of the pedal regulator is usually in bad condition and should be replaced.

Some Model B Ampico pianos are equipped with a subduing switch in the left panel of the drawer. This switch is similar to the Model A modifying switch, but it has only one alternate position. No mention of the subduing switch or its function is found in the 1929 manual. The function of this switch is described in detail below.

When the switch is moved to the "Subdued" position, suction is admitted to a tube which runs to the first intensity adjuster in the rear compartment of the piano. This tube leads into two pouches in the upper part of the adjuster block. These pouches (one for bass and one for treble) normally act as a shutoff, covering three holes. A sketch (see Figure 29) illustrates the layout of the area which is normally covered by one of the pouches. When the switch is at

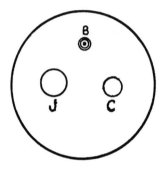

Fig. 29. Area Inside First Intensity Adjuster Covered by Subduing Mechanism Pouches

the "Subdued" position, vacuum pulls the two pouches away from their respective covered surfaces, and exposes the two holes beneath each pouch, as well as the bleed at the top of the sketch. These two holes becoming exposed act, in effect, as a connection between chamber C and point J of Figure 4 of the 1929 service manual.

Normally, there is a considerable vacuum differential between chamber C and point J when the piano is playing at high volume with the intensity valves closed, shutting off the atmosphere spilling into chamber C. However, the vacuum differential is not very great at low intensities, when the intensity valves are bleeding atmosphere into chamber

C and vacuum is passing through them and partially exhausting the tube at point J.

When the switch is at the "Subdued" position and the pouches are pulled back to connect chamber C with point J, this vacuum differential will be considerably reduced at high intensities by the atmosphere spilling into chamber C through the connection. This reduction of vacuum in chamber C will cause the pump suction in chamber G to pull the cloth farther across the grid B, thus reducing the suction reaching the pneumatic stack and consequently reducing the piano's maximum volume level. When the intensity valves open and the piano plays softly, the vacuum in chamber C drops, due to the atmosphere passing through the open intensity valves, and the vacuum at point J rises due to the open intensity valves allowing suction to pass to that point. This almost eliminates the vacuum differential between chamber C and point J. To eliminate the differential completely and thus make the piano play at its normal low-volume level even though the switch is at "Subdued," the suction bleed at the top of the sketch (Figure 29) admits just enough suction to raise the vacuum level at the connection to that of chamber C. This, in essence, means that at the higher intensities the piano's volume is reduced; but at its lowest intensities the playing remains normal. This is necessary to prevent its missing the very soft notes, which it would do if the entire volume level were reduced by a continuous atmospheric bleed. This subduing mechanism operates with no moving parts, and is a good example of the beautiful refinement of design which is embodied in the Model B Ampico action.

The DUO-ART

The Duo-Art reproducing piano operates on the principle of dividing music into theme and accompaniment. Other reproducing pianos simply divide their music into bass and treble sections, and control each side of the pneumatic stack by an individual expression regulator operated from its side of the music roll. The Duo-Art system utilizes two dissimilar expression controls, operated from different sides of the music roll.

Once the operation of the Duo-Art expression system is grasped, its simplicity will be evident. However, for the beginner, it is sometimes difficult to comprehend. A detailed description of its operation follows.

The division of Duo-Art music into theme and accompaniment is accomplished by the use of four expression tracks on each side of the music roll, plus one theme hole on each side. The four expression tracks appear as vertical elongated holes in the tracker bar, above the last four note holes in the bass and treble. The theme holes are horizontal elongated holes just beyond the ends of the row of note holes.

The four expression tracks on the treble end of the roll control the theme dynamics. The four on the bass end control the accompaniment dynamics.

When the piano is playing normally, the volume level of the entire pneumatic stack is controlled by the accompaniment expression mechanism, as long as no theme perforations are present in the roll. This is unlike other reproducing piano systems, in which the two sides of the stack are controlled separately all the time.

The function of the theme mechanism is to shift control of the individual sides of the stack instantaneously to the theme control tracks.

When a small theme perforation, usually shaped like a pair of typewritten ditto marks, appears over one of the theme holes in the tracker bar, it opens a valve which connects the suction in the theme expression regulator with the side of the stack controlled by the valve opened.

When the theme mechanism is in use, the stack is *divided*, as in other reproducing pianos. Each side of the stack is controlled by its individual tracker bar theme hole. Actually, there is a division between the sides of the stack at all times —but when the piano's playing is controlled by the accompaniment control tracks, the same suction is fed into both sides of the stack, so for practical purposes the stack is not divided when under accompaniment control.

In other words, the general volume level of the entire piano is normally controlled by the accompaniment tracks. When a sudden change in volume (e. g., an accented note) is demanded, the proper dynamic level is set up by the theme control tracks. Then, at the precise instant that the sudden change is needed, a small theme perforation (either in bass or treble) comes along. During the short instant that the theme perforation opens the theme hole in the tracker bar, the control of that particular side of the piano's stack is quickly shifted to the theme tracks. As soon as the theme hole has passed over the tracker bar, the entire piano is again controlled by the accompaniment tracks. The theme tracks are in control only as long as the theme hole is open. Thus, very high dynamic levels could be set up on the theme tracks and the piano could still be playing very softly, as long as there is no theme hole open.

Any high suction which may be generated in one side of the pneumatic stack is prevented from feeding back into the other side of the stack by a check valve in the theme expression mechanism. One side of the stack can thus be playing at fortissimo under theme control while the other side is playing at pianissimo under accompaniment control.

The theme and accompaniment tracks operate separate "accordion pneumatics" which control the position of a knife valve in the expression regulators. Illustration G on page 21 of the 1927 Duo-Art service manual presents a clear diagram of the moving parts of this mechanism. These accordion pneumatics consist of two sets of four pneumatic chambers of varying sizes. By exhausting various chambers of the accordion pneumatics, different stages of collapse of the pneumatics can be obtained. Thus, different playing levels of the piano are produced.

The mechanical construction of the parts of the Duo-Art expression system, together with a discussion of the dynamic gradations used, will be found in pages 15 through 21 of the 1927 Duo-Art service manual and need not be duplicated here.

The repairman should carefully check the action of the control levers at the front of the Duo-Art's key-bed. If any of their valves are leaking, or if binding or sticking in their action takes place, it will affect the performance of the piano. With a tube, check the tightness of the seals on the dynamic valve at the left of the key-bed, and of the bass and treble accent valves and the rewind pallet valve. These must seal their tubes completely when they are placed in the closed position. If trouble is detected, remove the pallets and replace their leather. Work the solo and accompaniment levers to detect any binding in their operation.

The Duo-Art accordion pneumatics should be removed and serviced before the test roll is used on the piano. The accordion pneumatics are easily removed by unscrewing the leather nut on the C-shaped rod on the top surface of each pneumatic, then removing the two screws holding the pneumatics to their mounting brackets. The accordion pneumatics will invariably need to be re-covered, as the factory originally used tan pouch leather on them, and this material does not hold up as well as pneumatic cloth when exposed to circulating air. The re-covering of these pneumatics is something of a ticklish business, and great care should be taken that it is done correctly. In the opinion of this writer, the easiest way to do the job is to make up small squares of wood which can be used as spacers between the five boards of the pneumatics when covering them. The four pieces of wood should be made about 2½" square, and should be ³⁄₁₆", ¼", ⅜", and ⅝" thick respectively. These will give the proper spacing to each board in the pneumatics. Tan pouch leather should be used to cover the pneumatics again, as it is flexible enough to provide no resistance to the operation of any segment of the pneumatics. It will last for at least twenty years, and no repairman should complain at having to re-cover a pneumatic once every twenty years! After the pneumatics are covered and the adjusting blocks re-attached, the gaps of the individual segments of the pneumatics should be precisely adjusted. The gaps should be ¹⁄₁₆", ⅛", ¼", and ½", and they are adjusted by turning the small hex-head screws in the wooden adjuster blocks. This should be done with a small wrench. Do not use pliers, as they have a distressing habit of slipping off the screw heads and puncturing the newly-covered pneumatics. Make these gap adjustments very carefully, as they are vital to the correct performance of the Duo-Art.

At this point, before proceeding with the test roll, the pump spill level must be checked. This is one of the fundamental adjustments of the action and must not be overlooked. Turn the "Duo-Art" lever in the spool box to the "On" position. Attach the vacuum gauge to some point between the pump and the expression regulating mechanism (a tee may have to be inserted temporarily in the main supply hose). Run the test roll to a point at which blank paper is covering the tracker bar. Set the dynamic switch at the left of the key-bed to its "Normal" position. Measure the suction with the pump running. It should read between 18″ and 20″. If this is not the case, the pump spill setting will have to be adjusted. On Duo-Art uprights this is accomplished by varying the setting of the spill valve arm, which is illustrated at point 4 of Illustration J, page 28, manual. On grands it is done by adjusting the arm which is being pulled by spring 8 in Illustration R, page 45, manual.

When the spill level has been regulated, begin running the test roll. The following information applies only to the Duo-Art test roll furnished by Player Piano Company or the other supply houses.

Test 1, tempo test. With the tempo at 70, the roll should travel from point 1 to point 2 in exactly one minute. If adjustment is necessary, vary the setting of spring 9 in Illustration M, page 35, manual. This illustration applies to grands as well as uprights. At this time, do not worry about the repetition of the individual notes, as this should be checked again after the expression adjustments are made.

Point 2 on the Duo-Art test roll is the end of test 1, so to eliminate confusion there is no test 2.

Test 3 checks the operation of the sustaining pedal (damper lift). Before making this test, the regulated pedal suction should be checked. On upright Duo-Arts this suction is controlled by the pedal regulator, shown in Illustration N, page 37, manual. On grands, it is controlled by the modulator pneumatic, shown in Illustration P, page 41, manual. The suction should be regulated, by adjusting the coil spring on the regulator pneumatic, to a level approximately two inches lower than the pump spill level. After this has been accomplished, check the operation of the sustaining pedal. The dampers should be lifted away from the strings approximately ⅛″, and they should lift evenly throughout the compass of the dampers. Adjustment of the lift is made on uprights by varying the setting of screw 2 in Illustration N, page 37, manual. On grands it is made either by varying the screw which adjusts the amount of collapse of pneumatic 9, Illustration Q, page 42, manual, or by varying the setting of the leather nuts on the linkage from this pneumatic to the damper action. The sustaining pedal action should operate quickly and smoothly. Some Duo-Art rolls were originally made with unusually small bridges between consecutive pedal perforations, and unless the sustaining pedal mechanism is in perfect condition the dampers will not be able to return to the strings and dampen them before the next pedal perforation comes along. The test roll will check this. The four consecutive perforations in Test 3 should completely raise the dampers, and then return them between each perforation with the roll running at tempo 70.

Test 4 checks the operation of the soft pedal. On uprights, the hammers should move to one inch from the strings when the pedal comes on. On grands with hammer rail lift, the hammers should rise to ⅝″ from their normal position. On grands with key action shift, the action should be shifted to the right just enough that the hammers strike only two of the strings in the tenor and treble trichord notes. This requires careful regulation of the piano action. On uprights the pedal travel can be adjusted by varying screw 3 in Illustration N, page 37, manual. On most grands the hammer rail lift is adjusted by varying the screw in the fixed deck of the soft pedal pneumatic which is located behind the spool box (and is difficult to reach). Usually Duo-Art grands with key action shift will require no adjustment on this mechanism, but if adjustment is necessary it can be accomplished by varying screw 6 in Illustration S, page 46, manual. As in the sustaining pedal test, the soft pedal should go completely off between the consecutive perforations in test 4 with the tempo at seventy.

Tests 5 and 6 are running tests of the accompaniment and solo accordion pneumatics. These tests merely check the operation of the pneumatics and their valves, and are not intended as regulation tests.

Test 7 is very important, as it checks the adjustment of the zero accompaniment level, which determines the adjustment of all the other intensity levels indirectly. Before making this test, a few preliminary adjustments should be made which are adequately described in the text following the heading "Test No. 7, Accompaniment Zero Setting" on page 23 of the service manual and which will not be repeated here. With the roll running at tempo eighty, the notes in the first two arpeggios should play very softly. If they do not play at all, or if they play too loudly, adjust screw 7 in Illustration F, page 18, manual. Be careful not to attempt to adjust screw 7 without first having loosened set screw 8, or the threads on screw 7 will be stripped. Very slight adjustments of screw 7 will cause considerable change in the zero level, so do not turn the screw much without checking the level again. Watch the position of the accompaniment regulator pneumatic—setting the zero level softer will cause it to open slightly, while increasing the level will cause the pneumatic to close a little.

When the zero level has been adjusted such that the notes

in test 7 play very softly, run the test roll through test 8 at tempo eighty. This arpeggio, played with the sustaining pedal off, should not play, or should play only an occasional note. This is due to the extra weight of the dampers which are now resting on their respective keys, rather than being held up by the sustaining pedal mechanism.

The goal in tests 7 and 8 is to set the accompaniment zero level so that the notes will play very softly in test 7 when the sustaining pedal raises their dampers, but will miss or skip most of the time in test 8 when the dampers' weight is on the keys. It should be emphasized again that this is an extremely important adjustment, and considerable time should be devoted to it, even though it may prove frustrating for a while.

Test 9 is a repetition of test 7, intended as a final check on the accompaniment zero setting.

Test 10 is similar in character to test 7, as the notes in the arpeggio should play softly. However, test 10 checks the theme zero setting, instead of the accompaniment. The notes in this test should play "one degree" louder than the notes in the accompaniment zero tests. Unfortunately, the Aeolian Company never did get around to defining precisely what one degree is supposed to mean, so the repairman must be guided by common sense. A vacuum gauge is a valuable tool in this test, as it can be used to adjust the theme level precisely. Using the vacuum gauge, the theme zero level should be set to approximately one inch higher suction than the accompaniment zero level. This can be done with the roll at rest. When checking the suction of the accompaniment zero level, run the roll until blank paper completely covers the tracker bar and attach the gauge to one of the tracker bar tubes (on grands it can be attached by pulling off one of the tracker tubes under the key bed, and on uprights it can be attached to one of the tubes at the lower front of the action). Measure the accompaniment suction carefully. Then run the roll until one of the theme perforations in test 10 opens a theme hole (if the gauge is connected to a bass tracker bar tube, open a bass theme hole, and vice versa). Adjust the theme suction one inch higher than the accompaniment suction. Adjustment is made similar to the accompaniment adjustment, but on the opposite side of the expression box. When this has been done, run the roll through test 10 at tempo eighty. All notes in the arpeggios should play softly, but none should miss or skip. If no vacuum gauge is available when making this test, the theme can be adjusted by ear to simply play slightly louder than the accompaniment; however, the use of a gauge is recommended.

Test 11 is similar in character to test 8, as it plays a quick arpeggio with the sustaining pedal off and the weight of the dampers resting on their keys. With the tempo at eighty, the notes in test 11 should miss or should barely play.

Tests 12 through 18 check the settings of the various accompaniment expression levels. This is done in much the same fashion as the zero theme and accompaniment levels were adjusted. Chords are played at each volume level, some of which should play softly and some of which should not play at all.

Test 12 is another check of the zero accompaniment level. The chords should not play with the roll running at tempo eighty.

The chords in test 13 should play very softly at the first

intensity level. If they do not play, adjust the hex screws on the topmost chamber of the accompaniment accordion pneumatic such that the chamber can collapse very slightly more. Repeat the test until the results are satisfactory.

The chords in test 14 should not play or should barely play. If they play audibly, the first intensity level is too high and the hex screws governing the topmost chamber of the accompaniment accordion pneumatic should be adjusted to prevent the chamber from collapsing quite so far.

The chords in test 15 should play softly at intensity level 2. If not, adjust the hex screws governing the second chamber of the accompaniment accordion pneumatic.

The chords in test 16 should not play or should barely play at intensity level 2. If adjustment is necessary, proceed as in test 15.

The chords in test 17 should play at intensity level 4. If not, adjust the hex screws on the third chamber of the accompaniment accordion pneumatic.

The chords in test 18 should not play or should barely play at intensity level 4. If adjustment is necessary, proceed as in test 17.

Test 19 plays four chords at intensity level 8. These chords should play loudly, and are not intended as regulating chords.

Test 20 plays four chords at the maximum accompaniment level. These chords should play extremely loudly, and are not intended as regulating chords.

Test 21 plays five chords at increasing intensity levels, not intended as regulating chords.

Tests 22 through 29 are exactly the same as tests 12 through 18, except that they check the theme intensity levels. Follow the instructions on the test roll sheet and adjust each theme accordion pneumatic chamber by varying the settings of the hex screws.

Tests 30 through 32 are identical to tests 19 through 21, and are not intended as regulating tests.

It should be emphasized here that the Duo-Art test roll—indeed, *any* reproducing piano test roll—provides only an approximate guide to adjusting and regulating its reproducing action. It is necessarily a sort of average of settings which have been found most suitable for most pianos. As such, it is usually an accurate and valuable tool for finishing off the adjustment of player actions. However, pianos are just as individual as humans are—and no one who has had experience working with Duo-Art actions can deny that they exhibit individual characteristics. Occasionally, an action will be met which will simply not perform properly when adjusted in conformance with the test roll.

When this happens, the simplest and most sensible solution to the problem is to adjust the action such that the piano sounds well! This is certainly the important criterion. None but a fool would doggedly adjust an action to rigid conformance with the test roll only to have this result in poor performance of the piano! With the Duo-Art, the recommended procedure is this: bring the action into strict accord with the test roll, using great care to get all the adjustments perfect. Then, play six or eight music rolls of various types. On eight out of ten pianos, no further adjustment will be necessary. If any trouble is present, its symptoms will probably be skipping or missing notes at low intensities: often ballad rolls will reveal this. These skipping notes can usually be eliminated by adjusting the theme and accompaniment zero levels upwards by one-half inch of suction. It is imperative to use a vacuum gauge for this adjustment. Then, play the roll or rolls in which the skipping notes were evident, and notice whether the malady has been corrected. In some cases, the zero levels may have to be adjusted upwards by one full inch of suction—but this is seldom necessary and should not be done until the need is plainly evident. A number of rolls should be played before any further adjustment is considered. The Aeolian Company technicians were none too careful in inserting expression perforations in Duo-Art rolls. This writer has seen dozens of instances in which insufficient expression tracks were opened for chords or arpeggios, with results that even the most perfectly-adjusted Duo-Art cannot cope with.

Duo-Art grands (except some early ones) came equipped with a crash valve, the operation of which is fully explained on page 44 of the service manual. It is mentioned here merely as a reminder that it should be checked and adjusted if necessary.

In 1904 the firm of Michael Welte & Son, located in Freiburg, Germany, announced that it had perfected a device for playing the piano known as the Welte-Mignon. This was the first major reproducing instrument marketed in the world. Most of the early German Welte-Mignon instruments were made in cabinet-player form, designed to play the keys of any piano to which they were attached.

In 1911 the Welte-Mignon was first manufactured in the United States. This American-made Welte-Mignon was made under the auspices of the German firm, and later became known as the "Licensee" Welte. The "Licensee" action was installed in American pianos, and during the late 1920's, Welte actions were available in one hundred and twelve makes of American instruments. In 1916 the Welte-Mignon "Licensee" agreement became the property of the Auto-Pneumatic Action Company, which manufactured Welte-Mignon actions until the early 1930's.

After the close of the First World War, there arose a firm called the Welte-Mignon Corporation, connected with the German firm, which brought onto the market a piano known as the "Original" Welte-Mignon. This was advertised as "The Welte-Built Welte-Mignon Reperforming Piano." Evidence points to the fact that these Welte pianos were actually built at the Estey Piano Company factory in New York City. Very early examples of these "Original" Welte instruments have drawers in which the rolls are placed while playing, as do the Welte "Licensee" pianos. However, most "Original" Welte instruments have the roll spool box above the keyboard, in the same position as the Duo-Art grand roll compartment. These "Original" Weltes can play the "Licensee" rolls, and have the same general expression system as all Welte-Mignon instruments.

The Welte-Mignon reproducing action is controlled by a very simple system of pneumatics which govern the suction reaching the pneumatic stack. The physical layout of these control pneumatics is illustrated in the drawing captioned "The Welte-Mignon Licensee Expression Device" in the Vestal Press reprint of the Welte-Mignon service manual. The Welte-Mignon employs the familiar "split" pneumatic stack (divided into bass and treble halves); hence there is a separate set of control pneumatics for the bass and treble parts of the music. The pneumatic at the top center of the abovementioned drawing, labeled Expression Pneumatic (B), is the main control pneumatic in the system. It controls, through linkage, the pneumatic at the bottom of the illustration, labeled "Governor Pneumatic," which contains a knife valve, similar to that which is used in all air-motor governors and which is also used in the Duo-Art expression system. The pneumatic at the top right, labeled "Stop Pneumatic" (but generally known as the "Mezzo-Forte Pneumatic"), locks the expression pneumatic halfway closed and thus keeps the piano playing at medium intensity. It can also be used as a softening device, as it can prevent the expression pneumatic from closing all the way and thus keep the piano from playing over half volume. Its main function, however, is to serve as a "reference point" for the expression pneumatic, which will be explained shortly.

The loudness of the Welte-Mignon piano is completely dependent upon the position of its main expression pneumatics. The farther these pneumatics are collapsed, the louder the piano plays. The position of these pneumatics is controlled by several valves, which admit suction or atmosphere to the pneumatics as the music roll expression perforations dictate. Most of these valves are of the lock-and-cancel type, unlike most valves found in reproducing pianos. This means that each valve uses two expression perforations—one to turn it on, and one to turn it off. This may be seen by referring to Cut A in the service manual, which shows the tracker bar expression scheme with two holes for most of the controls. The valves which operate the forzando control are not lock-and-cancel valves. These valves can be seen in Figure 26, near the center of the tubing charts furnished with the service manual.

For convenience' sake, the following explanations refer to only one expression unit: however, they apply to both.

The position of the main expression pneumatic is controlled by four tracker holes: crescendo on, crescendo off, forzando on, and forzando off. The crescendo on and off mechanism provides a means whereby the expression pneumatic can be gradually collapsed and re-opened. The forzando mechanism can exhaust and re-open the pneumatic instantaneously, providing a great change of volume level of the piano in a very short moment of time. The forzando is often used for giving sharp, heavy accents to notes, or to raise or lower the volume level of the piano quickly; while the crescendo mechanism is in use much of the time, to provide the normal changes of volume which most music rolls demand.

The crescendo mechanism is simply a valve which exhausts the expression pneumatic through an adjustable bleed. The adjusting screw for this bleed is shown as Screw I on the top of the Expression Pneumatic in the service manual drawing of the Welte-Mignon Expression Device. It is also illustrated as Screw P in Figures 1 through 4 on the tubing charts. By regulating this screw, the speed of collapse of the pneumatic can be varied. The crescendo "off" control consists of a smaller adjustable bleed which constantly connects the expression pneumatic to the atmosphere, and which allows the expression pneumatic to open itself gradually after it has been collapsed. This bleed is adjusted by turning the screw which restricts the "Crescendo Off" passage in the service manual drawing of the Expression Device (illustrated as Screw 0 in Figures 1 through 4 on the tubing charts).

The forzando "on" mechanism consists of another valve which exhausts the expression pneumatic at a very rapid rate. This is also adjustable. However, in this detail, variance is found between different Welte-Mignon actions; for some actions have two means of adjusting the forzando, while others have only one. The action illustrated in the Vestal Press reprint of the service manual has only one means of adjustment. The adjusting screw is designated as "Forzando regulating screw N" in Figure 9 on the tubing charts. This screw restricts the travel of the forzando valve, thus regulating the amount of suction which passes through it. On Welte actions with two types of forzando adjustment, there is an adjusting screw which governs the size of passage J in the drawing of the Expression Device. The forzando speed can be roughly adjusted with the valve's regulating screw, then finely adjusted with the screw governing passage J.

The forzando "off" control consists of a simple valve which controls two pouches. These two pouches, when actuated, admit atmosphere to the expression pneumatic and the regulator pneumatic, and thus instantaneously reduce the level of the piano to its minimum. These two pouch units are located on top of the Expression Pneumatic and the Governor Pneumatic, as shown on the service manual drawing of the Welte Expression Device.

The mezzo-forte pneumatic, as has already been said, can lock the expression pneumatic in the halfway-closed position, thus keeping the piano playing at half volume; or it can be used to soften the piano by preventing the expression pneumatic from closing entirely. Its main function, however, is to serve as a reference point for the expression pneumatic. The Welte-Mignon employs a peculiar "floating" expression system. Unlike the Ampico and Duo-Art systems, the Welte employs no definite steps of volume increase. In the Welte system, very small discrepancies in the adjustment of the various speeds of opening and closing the expression pneumatic can accumulate into an appreciable error in the volume level of the piano. Therefore, the Welte designers intended the mezzo-forte pneumatic to return the expression pneumatic to a definite stage or level at periodic points throughout the music roll. This could have been done by allowing the expression pneumatic to return to its rest position, or by collapsing it all the way—but the musical results would have been quite disagreeable. Since the piano plays much of the time at approximately half volume, the halfway-closed position of the expression pneumatic is the most logical point at which to establish a reference.

The soft pedal and sustaining pedal controls are also of the lock-and-cancel type. The valves which control these mechanisms are illustrated in Figure 6 of the tubing charts.

Before beginning the process of testing and adjusting the Welte-Mignon player action, some preliminary work is advisable. First, the repairman should determine whether the piano is to be used exclusively for playing Welte rolls, or whether 88-note rolls will also be used on it. If the instrument is to be used for Welte rolls only, it is suggested that the 88-note control lever linkage be removed from the piano. This is particularly important on grands, as the sliding sleeves which extend the control levers habitually stick and prevent the drawer from closing smoothly. So as not to alter the appearance of the drawer, just the portion of the sliding sleeve which is fastened to the back of the piano can be removed, leaving the control levers intact in the drawer. When removing this sliding sleeve, also remove its attached linkage which pulls the Expression Pneumatic closed as the drawer levers are pressed together. When removing this linkage, a fair-sized hole may be exposed, leading from atmosphere into the interior of the Expression Pneumatic. This hole should be tightly sealed with a piece of heavy pneumatic cloth and a little glue. It must be emphasized that removal of these parts is optional, even if the piano is to be used for Welte rolls exclusively: but their removal is recommended, as it eliminates a source of constant trouble and results in a better-operating Welte action. The "Original" Welte-Mignon instruments do not have these control levers, so the repairman need give them no concern when working on this type of piano.

A final check before beginning the test roll adjustments is advisable. The position of the mezzo-forte lock hooks (see Figure 1 on the tubing charts) on the bass and treble mezzo-forte pneumatics should be carefully checked and set if necessary. The mezzo-forte lock hook on the bass pneumatic should be exactly $\frac{7}{16}''$ from the prong on the moving deck of the main expression pneumatic with the piano turned off. On the treble pneumatic it should be $\frac{1}{2}''$ from the hook on the expression pneumatic. Hold the mezzo-forte pneumatic in the collapsed position when checking these adjustments, which are important and should be adjusted with care.

Some Welte actions were built with a small piece of tan pouch leather attached to both surfaces of the mezzo-forte lock hooks. If this has deteriorated, it should be replaced: however, if none was originally present, do not put any there. Be sure to place a small quantity of graphite grease on both surfaces of the mezzo-forte lock hooks, whether or not leather is present.

The following instructions apply to the Welte-Mignon test roll furnished by Player Piano Company and the other piano supply houses. All tests should be made with the Welte switch lever in the "on" position and the volume control in the "loud" position.

Test 1 on the Welte test roll is the replay notch. On all Welte-Mignon actions constructed after approximately 1923, the repeat mechanism is controlled by a hole in the takeup spool. However, test rolls are furnished with this replay notch to check Welte actions made before 1923.

Test 2 checks the minimum playing level of the bass and

treble. The notes should sound at their softest level, but should not miss or skip. Adjustment is made by turning the leather nuts on the rods connecting the Expression Pneumatic and the Governor Pneumatic, shown as H in the service manual drawing of the Expression Device. See Figure 1 on the tubing charts, and page 8 of the manual.

Test 3 checks the action of each note. All notes should speak softly. If any note does not speak, check the operation of the valve, pneumatic, and piano action. See pages 8 and 9 of the service manual for details.

Test 3-A is the tempo test. With the tempo lever at 80, exactly one minute should elapse between the two notes marked X. For adjustment procedure, see the service manual, page 9.

At this point, the repairman should remember that *all* expression tests *must* be made at a tempo of precisely 80. Any small variations from this tempo will result in large inaccuracies in the expression of the piano. When adjusting an Ampico or Duo-Art, the tempo can be approximate and the adjustments will not be affected; but in the Welte, it must be completely accurate or the performance of the piano will be grossly incorrect.

In test 4 UP, the crescendo pneumatic hook should contact the mezzo-forte lock hook at the precise instant that the note is struck. If adjustment is necessary, it is accomplished by turning screw P (see Figures 1 through 4 on the tubing charts) very carefully. If the hooks contact too soon, screw P should be turned in; and if they contact too late, the screw should be turned outward. Do not move the screw more than a quarter of a turn at one time.

Test 4 DOWN checks the speed of return of the crescendo pneumatic. After the pneumatic has collapsed in test 4 UP, it should return to rest at the precise instant the note is struck. If adjustment is necessary, it may be made by turning screw O (see Figures 1 through 4 on the tubing charts), which varies the pneumatic's permanent bleed to atmosphere. If adjustment is necessary on screw O, it will be necessary to perform test 4 UP over again, as turning screw O affects the regulation of screw P.

The regulation of tests 4 UP and 4 DOWN is a matter of careful adjustment between screws O and P. Considerable patience and care must be exercised in making these adjustments, as they are probably the most important adjustments in the entire piano. If regulating a grand piano, it is helpful to have a second person run the roll back and forth while the repairman makes the adjustments underneath the piano.

Test 5 checks the operation of the forzando. In this test, the hook on the expression pneumatic should rise to a position exactly in line with the mezzo-forte lock hook, and should then return to its rest position immediately. If this is not the case, the forzando will need adjusting. As has been stated before, Welte actions differ in the methods of adjusting the forzando. Some actions have two adjustments, some only one. On actions with two adjustments, test 5 should be accomplished by varying the setting of screw N in Figure 9 of the tubing charts for the rough adjustment of the forzando, then using the screw which controls the size of passage J in the drawing of the Expression Device for the fine adjustment. On actions which have only one forzando adjustment, the entire operation is performed with screw N in Figure 9.

If tests 4 UP and 4 DOWN have been made carefully, the only thing that can possibly require adjusting in test 5 is the forzando mechanism, and screws O and P should not be touched, inasmuch as they are crescendo regulating screws. If the setting of these two screws is accidentally disturbed, tests 4 UP and 4 DOWN must be made again.

Test 6 is of the same nature as test 5, only the expression pneumatic should rise to a point about a quarter of an inch above the mezzo-forte pneumatic hook. If test 5 has been made correctly, no adjustment of the forzando should be required in test 6.

Test 7 is another test similar to tests 5 and 6, but this time the expression pneumatic should collapse completely. While the pneumatic is being held completely collapsed, a note will be struck. Immediately following this note, the pneumatic should instantly open to its fullest extent, at which time three notes will be struck in quick succession. The three notes should be played at the softest playing level. If this is not correct, then the forzando "off" mechanism is not operating properly and will need attention. This mechanism consists of two pouches (mounted on top of both large pneumatics shown in the service manual drawing of the Welte Expression Device) which instantaneously spill the expression pneumatic and its regulator pneumatic to atmosphere, causing them to spring open very quickly. Improper operation of this device is usually caused by trouble in the forzando "off" valve, or defective pouch units on the pneumatics.

Test 8 checks the expression pneumatic in conjunction with the mezzo-forte pneumatic. In this test, the mezzo-forte pneumatic should collapse, and the expression pneumatic should rise until its hook rests against the lock hook of the mezzo-forte pneumatic. The action of these pneumatics should be simultaneous, but the mezzo-forte pneumatic should be collapsed before the expression pneumatic reaches its mid-point. In other words, the expression pneumatic hook should not miss the mezzo-forte lock hook. While the pneumatics are in the collapsed position, a note will be struck at medium intensity. Immediately after the note strikes, the two pneumatics should return to their rest positions, at which time two more notes should be struck softly. If these latter two notes are struck at a level above minimum intensity, the forzando "off" mechanism should be given attention as outlined in test 7.

Test 9 is supposed to test the evenness of playing of the bass and treble sides of the pneumatic stack. The expression pneumatics and mezzo-forte pneumatics lock themselves at the medium intensity, then a note is struck on either side of the stack. The notes should sound with equal loudness (providing the piano action and hammers are in good condition). If all preliminary adjusting has been done correctly, no trouble should be experienced. If, however, the notes do not sound equally, return to test 1 and check the minimum intensity level. Also check the position of the mezzo-forte hooks as outlined earlier in this section.

Test 10 is one of the most important tests, as it checks the quick action of the forzando mechanism. The expression pneumatic makes six gradual steps upward until it reaches a point at which its hook is exactly even with the mezzo-forte hook. If test 5 has been made correctly, there should be little trouble with this test. However, if adjustment is necessary, it should be made by turning screw N in Figure 9 of the tubing charts on Welte actions which have two adjustments for the forzando speed. If adjusting an action with only one forzando adjustment, the setting of screw N should have been correctly determined in test 5 and should require no changing. "Original" Welte pianos have an adjusting screw which varies the size of the bleed F in Figure 9, and this is useful in making test 10. Turning this screw inward will make the expression pneumatic climb upward farther, and vice versa (do not move the screw more than a tiny fraction of a turn at one time).

Test 11 is simply a series of quick repetitions of the expression pneumatic, and serves no purpose other than to check the operation of the forzando on and off controls.

Test 12 runs the expression pneumatic to its highest point, then gives it a series of quick repetitions before returning it quickly to rest. This test also serves as a check on the operation of the pneumatic and the forzando controls.

Test 13 checks the operation of the mezzo-forte pneumatic. With the expression pneumatic hook firmly locked by the mezzo-forte pneumatic hook, the spring on the mezzo-forte pneumatic should pull the pneumatic open when its suction is cut off. In this test, the mezzo-forte and expression pneumatics lock together, and after a moment perforation 1 crosses the tracker bar and cuts off the suction to the mezzo-forte pneumatic, while the suction in the expression pneumatic remains on. The spring in the mezzo-forte pneumatic should open the pneumatic under these conditions. If this is not the case, remove the spring on the mezzo-forte pneumatic and strengthen it by bending it apart. As has been stated before, a little graphite grease should always be kept on both sides of the mezzo-forte lock hook to facilitate its sliding off the expression pneumatic hook.

Test 14 checks the operation of the soft pedal. The first check is completed with no notes being struck. The second time the hammer rail lifts, three notes are struck. Then the hammer rail returns to rest, when three more notes are struck. These three-note chords check the speed of operation of the hammer rail. When the first three notes strike, the hammer rail should be entirely lifted; and when the second three strike, the rail should be completely at rest. If this is not so, the action of the rail will have to be speeded up. In some cases this must be done by removing the soft pedal valve block (block F in Figure 26 of the tubing charts, and also Figure 6 of the charts) and, after disassembling the valve block, screwing the two valve surfaces slightly closer together to give the valve a bit more travel. Naturally, before going to this extent, check the obvious possibilities of a pinched hose or a punctured pedal pneumatic.

Test 15 is similar in character to test 14, but it applies to the sustaining pedal. The dampers are lifted twice from the strings to check the function of the pedal unit. Then, four notes are successively struck to determine the action of the damper return. The dampers should mute the strings the moment the expression perforation 7 crosses the tracker bar. After this, four notes are struck in succession to determine the speed of lift of the dampers. The notes are struck an instant after perforation 8 turns on the pedal, and they should sound until perforation 7 drops the dampers again. If the pedal action is sluggish, proceed as outlined in test 14.

Between test 15 and test 16, the test roll contains a few minutes of various kinds of music. Numerous notes are struck to check accenting capability of the action, and the expression mechanism is put through its paces. By watching the music roll and listening carefully to the notes, the repairman can tell whether everything is operating well.

121

Test 16 checks the operation of the sustaining pedal when playing 88-note rolls on the Welte-Mignon. The "Transforming Lever" should be turned to the "Welte Off" position, and the sustaining pedal switch should be turned on.

Test 17 checks the rewind mechanism when playing 88-note rolls. This test should also be made with the Transforming Lever at "Off."

Test 18 checks the rewind mechanism when playing Welte-Mignon rolls. The Transforming Lever must be in the "Welte On" position when making this test. The mechanism which is connected with the Welte Transforming Lever is adequately diagrammed in Figures 12 and 12A of the tubing charts, and will not be treated further here.

It cannot be repeated too often that the reproducing piano action is a precision instrument and must be treated as such. No amount of hasty work or "patch-up" work can produce a good job on a reproducing piano. The repairman who takes the trouble to understand thoroughly the action on which he is working, and who does a careful job of rebuilding, testing, and adjusting the mechanism, will be amply rewarded. A perfectly-operating Ampico, Duo-Art, or Welte-Mignon action installed in a fine-quality piano can produce amazingly good results. And the same reproducing action installed in the same piano can give forth terrible performances if it has been improperly or incompetently restored!

NICKELODEONS

As STATED in the preface to this book, the section on the nickelodeon is not long. Nickelodeons, for the most part, are not much more difficult to rebuild than ordinary player pianos; and inasmuch as the section of this book dealing specifically with tracker scales includes the necessary information to enable one to re-tube most of the nickelodeons which are commonly found, there seems to be no necessity for including detailed information on their repair, which would be repetition of what has been said in earlier chapters. As is the case with 88-note player pianos, so many varieties of nickelodeons exist that it would be impossible to give specific descriptions of the work necessary to rebuild each and every model. Thus, this section deals only with the special features of nickelodeons which are not found in 88-note players or reproducing pianos.

Approximately sixty-five makes of nickelodeons appeared on the American market between 1898 and 1930. Of this number, only a handful of brands attained anything approaching large-scale sales. The names which are the most familiar to the present-day collector of nickelodeons are:

Coinola, Cremona, Link, Nelson-Wiggen, Seeburg, Western Electric, and Wurlitzer. These seven brands probably accounted for over seventy-five per cent of all nickelodeons sold in America. Inasmuch as these are the machines most likely to come to the attention of the collector or rebuilder, they are discussed briefly in this chapter.

A large number of nickelodeons made by the above manufacturers were built to take standardized music rolls, and a discussion of these is included in the following paragraphs.

Probably the most common kind of nickelodeon roll was the A roll. These were produced by a number of companies to fit nickelodeons of many types and models. A rolls were perforated on a scale using six perforations per inch of width (known as six-to-the-inch among collectors), and their overall width was 11¼ inches. They were generally cut with ten tunes per roll, and were wound on cores having a 3½ inch inside diameter. They were instrumented without percussive effects, and were capable of playing up to two instruments in addition to the piano (i. e., mandolin, and either xylophone or pipes). Generally speaking, if a nickelodeon has a tracker bar with holes ⅛″ wide, with a paper track of 11¼″, and the machine plays three instruments or less (including the piano), it takes an A roll.

The other widely-used six-to-the-inch music roll of 11¼″ width was the G roll. To the inexperienced eye, G rolls can easily be mistaken for A rolls, as there is no external difference between the two types. If the roll in question has its original program label on it, the type can be immediately discerned from the roll number. In general, A roll numbers are merely digits, but G roll numbers are prefixed with the letter

G or the symbol 4X, depending upon the maker of the roll. Should the label be missing, the roll type can be discerned by unwinding the roll to its first perforation, a long slot which throws the roll drive gears from rewind to play position. This slot is very near the center of the paper on G rolls, while on A rolls it is close to the edge. The same applies to the shutoff perforation, which is close to the edge of A rolls but in the center of G rolls. G rolls contain a number of percussion control perforations, as well as perforations which turn various extra instruments on and off. Hence they are capable of operating machines of the orchestrion type. In general, any nickelodeon with tracker bar holes of ⅛" width, with a paper track of 11¼", and which contains four to twelve instruments, uses G rolls. The two biggest users of G rolls were Seeburg and Nelson-Wiggen.

When speaking of O rolls, the Coinola name immediately comes to mind, as this brand of nickelodeon was the foremost user of this type of roll. O rolls were perforated nine-to-the-inch, the same as regular 88-note piano rolls. They were also 11¼" wide, but were wound onto cores which were smaller than the A and G roll cores. Owing to their smaller perforation size, O rolls could contain a much wider variety of musical and percussive effects than most other nickelodeon rolls. They contain a large number of control perforations which turn various extra instruments on and off. They also have a special solo section in the music which enables certain instruments (usually xylophone or pipes) to play solo effects against the accompaniment of the piano. O rolls are generally among the best nickelodeon rolls produced, and they are considered quite desirable among collectors.

Closely akin to the O roll is the M roll, made specifically to fit the Cremona Style M Orchestrion. These rolls have a few more percussion perforations and instrument control perforations than the O roll. They are also cut on the nine-to-the-inch scale, and are 11¼″ wide.

Among the seven leading manufacturers of nickelodeons, only two, Link and Wurlitzer, produced their own music rolls for their instruments. Link made three types of rolls, the Link RX, Link C, and the Link A. Link A rolls are completely unrelated to regular A rolls. Link RX rolls fill the place of regular A rolls on Link pianos, as they are perforated to operate up to three instruments (including piano). Link C rolls are the same as RX rolls, but contain classical music. The Link A rolls were produced to play on Link orchestrions, which generally contain eight instruments. Link was the only major manufacturer to use an endless roll, and for this reason Link rolls are not wound onto cores as are regular nickelodeon rolls. They are 12″ wide and are perforated on the six-to-the-inch scale.

The Wurlitzer Company produced six varieties of rolls for use in their nickelodeons: they are; Pianino rolls, Automatic Player Piano rolls, Mandolin PianOrchestra rolls, Concert PianOrchestra rolls, Mandolin Quartette and Sextette rolls, and Player Harp rolls. These types were used only on nickelodeons, and should not be confused with the four varieties of band organ rolls which Wurlitzer produced. The Pianino was the smallest nickelodeon Wurlitzer manufactured, having only forty-four playing notes. Its rolls are 5½″ wide, and were issued in two forms, one being five- or six-tune rolls wound onto small spools with steel pin ends, and the other being ten-tune rolls with hollow cores to take interchangeable spools. Pianino rolls were perforated with several control slots to operate extra instruments, as well as a percussion hole for a snare drum, although these were not included in the simpler Pianinos which contained only piano and mandolin.

The "work-horse" rolls of the Wurlitzer nickelodeon family were Automatic Player Piano rolls, known among collectors as Wurlitzer 65-note rolls or Wurlitzer orchestra rolls. These rolls are 11%6″ wide, and contain enough control slots to operate several instruments, as well as bass and snare drums. These rolls were produced in two types, as were the Pianino rolls. One type was a regular ten-tune roll wound onto a core and using an interchangeable spool. The other type was a five-tune roll which was designed for use on the Wurlitzer automatic roll changer, a device which held six rolls and could automatically play through them in succession. Automatic Player Piano rolls were used on all Wurlitzer instruments which had keyboards.

The largest Wurlitzer nickelodeons were the Pian-Orchestras, large upright instruments without keyboards. These were made in quite a variety of styles and models. The smaller PianOrchestras used Mandolin PianOrchestra rolls, which were capable of controlling more instruments than the Automatic Player Piano rolls, and which were instrumented with several percussive effects. These rolls were 8⅞″ wide, and were wound onto small cores to take interchangeable spools. Concert PianOrchestra rolls were used on the biggest instruments, and these contained even more control slots and percussion than the Mandolin Pian-Orchestra rolls. Instruments which can play either of these types of rolls are considered highly desirable by collectors today.

Even more rare and desirable are the Wurlitzer Mandolin

Quartette and Mandolin Sextette, which produce music in imitation of mandolins, as their name implies. These both operate from the same type of roll.

The following paragraph is an outline of which music rolls fit which nickelodeons. To the advanced collector, this information may seem unworthy of inclusion here: however, as is stated plainly in its preface, this book is written for the beginner in the field of player instrument repair. The following paragraph may be of use to new collectors who acquire a machine without rolls and are faced with the task of acquiring some; or it may also enable a repairman to select the proper tracker tubing scale when preparing to re-tube a nickelodeon.

Coinola machines use A, C, and O rolls. Coinolas with tracker bar holes ⅛″ wide, and three instruments or less, use A rolls: those with nine tracker holes per inch of width, and three instruments, use C rolls (these are rare). Coinolas with four or more instruments take O rolls. Cremona nickelodeons take A or M rolls. Cremonas with tracker holes ⅛″ wide and three instruments or less use A rolls, while the orchestrions use M rolls with nine-to-the-inch spacing. Link pianos use Link RX or C rolls while orchestrions with four or more instruments use Link A rolls. Nelson-Wiggen pianos use A and G rolls: machines with three instruments or less take A rolls, those with four instruments or more use G rolls. Exactly the same thing applies to Seeburg machines, which use A and G rolls with the exception of the largest Seeburg orchestrion, the Style H, which uses special H rolls approximately 15 inches wide. Seeburg also made a Style X nickelodeon which was a sort of semi-reproducing instrument using XP rolls, but few of these exist. Western Electric machines use A rolls, although evidence points to the fact that Western Electric may have produced a very few machines using G rolls. If a Western Electric nickelodeon with four or more instruments exists, it would use G rolls: however, this writer has never encountered one. Wurlitzer Pianinos use Pianino rolls. All keyboard Wurlitzers use Automatic Player Piano rolls, whether they are simple piano-mandolin instruments or are of the orchestrion type. The large PianOrchestras use either Mandolin PianOrchestra or Concert PianOrchestra rolls, while the Mandolin Quartette and Mandolin Sextette use Mandolin Quartette rolls.

Nickelodeons which play only piano and mandolin contain no mechanisms which are much different from those found in regular 88-note players. However, the more elaborate machines often contain instruments, such as a snare drum and a xylophone, which are operated by repeating strikers. These repeating devices are constructed in several different ways, and a brief description of their operation is apropos.

Figure 30 represents a repeating pneumatic such as is used in Link pianos. Deck A is the fixed deck, while deck B is the movable deck; an external spring acts to hold these decks apart (spring not shown). When a vacuum is introduced through tube D, the pneumatic will start to collapse. As B moves toward A, E—which is a piece of wood hinged with leather at its lower end—will be caused to move toward A. The wooden rod at the top of E will then force valve C open, which tends to spill the vacuum, but in the meanwhile the opening from D will have been closed by the pad on the A

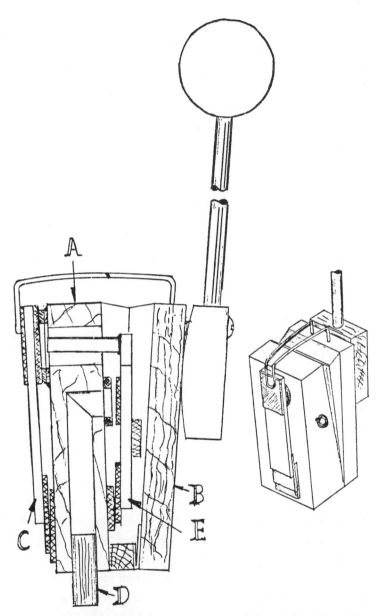

Fig. 30. Repeating Mechanism, as used in the *LINK* Coin-operated Piano

side of piece E, so that the main supply to the chest will not be lost through this opening. As soon as the vacuum is gone from the pneumatic, the spring tension will act to move B away from A, and the process then repeats itself in rapid succession. A beater attached to a striker arm is made to act upon a drum, xylophone, or other percussion instrument. Note that the beater is attached to B in such a manner that the clearance between the beater itself and the instrument it plays upon is readily adjustable by rocking the fitting. In the Link piano, these pneumatics are $1\frac{1}{4}$ inches wide; the illustration here is full scale.

A cross-section of a second type of repeating mechanism is shown in Figure 31. In this type of mechanism, the repetition is caused by rapid operation of a regular pneumatic valve, in contrast to the mechanism described in the preceding paragraph which is fed a constant suction supply from an external valve. In Figure 31, the repetition of the pneumatic is accomplished by alternately opening and closing the passage from the tracker bar to the pouch which controls the valve. This is performed by the sliding wooden block on the upper surface of the valve block. The slider has a hollow center which serves as an air passage, alternately connecting and disconnecting the two channels leading up to the top of the valve block. When the pneumatic is in its rest position and fully opened, the slider is positioned such that air can flow from the channel coming from the tracker bar into the channel leading to the pouch chamber. This will allow the pouch to rise and operate the valve, thus actuating the pneumatic. When the pneumatic reaches a certain point in its travel, the lower surface of the slider will close off the channel leading to the pouch, thus breaking the flow of air. This will cause the pouch and valve to drop, and the pneumatic will open. As it opens, the slider is pulled back to its former position, which allows air to flow through both channels, and the process begins over again.

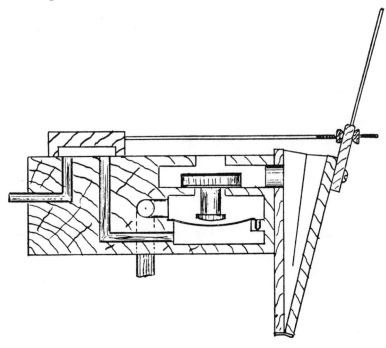

Fig. 31. Another Type of Repeating Mechanism

Almost every nickelodeon has some provision for operating the damper rail to produce sustaining pedal effect and the hammer rail to produce softness in the music. Also, nickelodeons which contain extra instruments have provision for turning these instruments on and off automatically. These mechanisms vary considerably from piano to piano, and depend, in their operation, upon what type of perforations in the music roll actuate them. Some of these devices are simply a valve which actuates a pneumatic; however, some of them are fairly complex. Generally, those which operate from long chain perforations in the music roll are of the single valve type: for example, the A roll actuates its mandolin bar, third instrument (xylophone or pipes), soft pedal and sustaining pedal by means of long chain perforations which simply keep the respective valves open for the proper length of time. Mechanisms of the lock-and-cancel type are sometimes more difficult to understand and to service. These are operated by two separate perforations in the tracker bar, one of which turns the particular unit on, and the other of which cancels it, or turns it off. Sometimes these consist of a pneumatic which pulls a rod to turn the instrument on, then is latched into this position by a ratchet tooth until a second pneumatic is actuated to release the ratchet tooth, at which time the first pneumatic is free to open again. However, these lock-and-cancel systems sometimes consist of valves which lock themselves in the "on" position until they are released by a second perforation. Each manufacturer produced different varieties of these actuator mechanisms, and it is impossible to generalize on their construction or operation. Occasionally rolls will use a combination of the extended chain perforation system and the lock-and-cancel system: for example, G rolls use extended chain perforations to operate the mandolin bar, soft pedal, and sustaining pedal, while all other instrument control is accomplished by means of lock-and-cancel mechanisms. For an explanation and illustration of several lock-and-cancel systems, the reader is referred to the service manuals for the Ampico and Welte-Mignon reproducing pianos, both of which use this type of mechanism. The Welte is entirely operated by lock-and-cancel devices, while the Ampico uses a combination of extended perforations and lock-and-cancel mechanism.

A word should be said about the tuning of nickelodeons which contain extra instruments. In most cases, these are fixed-pitch instruments, such as a xylophone, or instruments whose pitch range cannot be varied much, such as flute or violin pipes. In this case, the tuning of the piano is extremely important. In nickelodeons which contain only piano and mandolin, the piano does not necessarily need to be tuned to standard pitch, for it will sound all right as long as each string is in tune with the other strings. However, in nickelodeons which contain a xylophone or pipes, the piano must be tuned to the standard pitch to which the xylophone bars or pipes were originally tuned. This, in most cases, necessitates tuning the piano to A-435, which was the international standard pitch at the time most nickelodeons were built. All too few collectors seem to be conscious of the fact that nothing sounds worse than a nickelodeon in which the piano is playing flatter than the xylophone or pipes!

The flat leather belting which was originally used to drive the pump on certain nickelodeons (Link, Nelson-Wiggen, and Western Electric, to name a few) can be replaced with V-belting. If the pulley on the electric motor is replaced with a V-belt pulley, the new belt can be used on the pump pulley in place of the flat belt, providing the motor pulley is lined up with the pump pulley correctly.

REED ORGANS

REBUILDING THE PLAYER PIANO

FROM THE EARLY nineteenth century till the First World War, foot-powered reed organs were commercially available as musical instruments for the home and church. During the Victorian era they rivaled, if not surpassed, the piano as the basic musical instrument around which the family clustered in the evening and sang familiar songs. Reed organs and melodeons were manufactured in vast numbers in this country, and in a great variety of sizes and shapes. From the tiny portable folding organs through the parlor-sized melodeons to the towering, elaborate, gingerbread creations which adorn some of the more expensive reed organs, these instruments were available to suit the taste and pocketbook of every economic class.

Keyboard reed instruments, in spite of their huge variety of size and appearance, operate substantially alike. In almost every instrument, the depression of a key actuates linkage which opens a valve, which in turn admits either suction or pressure to a reed. This starts the reed tongue vibrating, which produces audible sound. Figure 32 is a diagram of a typical reed organ mechanism. The air is supplied by good-sized bellows which operate from foot pedals. The smaller reed instruments often have no stops or other controls to vary the volume or sound of the music they produce. Most melodeons have only one foot pedal which operates bellows, while the other pedal actuates swell shutters which give some control over the loudness of the music. Occasionally a melodeon will be found with a few stops, to vary the music a little; but these stops are primarily found on the larger upright reed organs. The stops sometimes actuate different sets of reeds, and operate mechanism which varies the sound of each individual set of reeds. Often tremolo effects are available, as well as octave couplers which enable the organist to further vary his music. However, despite the wide assortment of gadgets which were built into the larger and more expensive instruments, the basic principle of all keyboard reed instruments can be boiled down to a key-actuated valve admitting air to a reed.

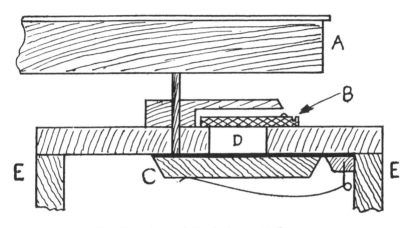

Fig. 32. A Typical Reed Organ Mechanism

A—Organ Key   D—Windway to reed
B—Reed   E—Wind chest
C—Pallet

Reed organs are found in various stages of repair. Sometimes organs will play well except for certain notes, which either will not speak or else play all the time. In this case, perhaps all that is needed is cleaning of the reeds for the organ to work reasonably well. Other organs may play on all the keys, but not enough air can be pumped up to operate them properly; and in this case the bellows probably need to be re-covered. Quite a variety of maladies affect reed organs, and the repairman will have to use a little ingenuity to diagnose the trouble correctly. Of course, sometimes organs need to be completely restored, in which case the repairman need not trouble himself trying to decide which part to fix, since he will wind up fixing them all!

If the large supply bellows in the organ are in need of re-covering, this should be the first step of the restoration.

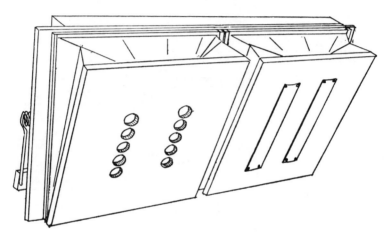

Fig. 33. A Reed Organ Bellows

Little testing can be done unless the bellows operate properly. In the case of vacuum bellows, the covering procedure is exactly the same as that used for covering the large supply bellows in the bottom of an upright player piano. Rather than repeat this information here, the reader is referred to that portion of this book. Since these bellows are generally large, spring-loaded ones, it is usually wise to leave a small strip of the old fabric on the bellows halfway along the open end, to keep the two bellows boards together while the springs are inside them. If all the old fabric has been removed, a small strip of new bellows cloth can be glued and tacked into position to do the job. Heavy bellows cloth, generally twill cloth impregnated with rubber, is used on supply bellows. Before applying the new cloth, the repairman should check the condition of the interior flap valves, and replace them if they have become rotten or warped.

Some reed organs operate on air pressure, rather than suction, and the supply bellows in instruments of the pressure type must be covered using somewhat different procedures. Pressure bellows contain stiffeners, called gussets, which prevent the sides of the bellows from puffing outward when pressure is created inside them. These gussets are usually made of cardboard, and are glued inside the bellows in such fashion that they maintain the flatness of the bellows surfaces and prevent the fabric from assuming its natural shape under pressure. These gussets must be replaced when the new fabric is applied to the bellows. For this reason, care should be taken in removing the old fabric, and it should be removed in one piece as far as is possible, so it can be used as a pattern. The new cloth should be cut to the exact dimensions of the old material, so it can be placed in its position on the bellows boards without having stray edges or overlaps. If the old gussets can be removed from the fabric without ruining them, they can be re-used; but if they must be damaged in removing them, new ones should be made from cardboard or some other material of approximately the same stiffness. The gussets should then be glued onto the new fabric in exactly the same position they occupied on the old fabric. This is an important step and should be done with extreme care. After the glue has dried, the new cloth can then be applied to the bellows boards in the usual manner. All glue should be permitted to become thoroughly dry before the bellows are tested, as it is a disgusting job to have to tear off newly-applied fabric to repair a gusset which has fallen off inside the bellows.

When replacing the re-covered bellows in the organ, it is a good idea to check the condition of the pedal straps. Often these have become rotten and are on the verge of breaking. If new ones are necessary, they can be made of cotton strapping such as upholsterers use for holding springs in place.

After the bellows have been reconditioned, the repairman can turn his attention to the upper portion of the instrument, which contains the reeds. It is generally a good idea to remove the reeds and check them for dirt, warping, or breakage. Many reed organs originally came equipped with a reed puller, which is often still inside the instrument, hanging on a small thong of leather or perhaps on a wooden bracket. If this is present, it should be used. If not, one must be made. A suitable puller can be improvised out of a nail or a small piece of steel. [Figure 34 shows the shape of a commercially-made reed puller.] Organ reeds have small notches across their ends, into which the reed puller hook is fitted. The individual reeds are drawn out of their slots with a straight, horizontal pulling motion. To prevent mix-ups, only one reed should be removed at a time, and it should be cleaned and replaced before the next one is removed. An incredible amount of dirt and dust can become lodged in reed tongues, and a check of each reed will reveal any such matter, which should be removed with a pen-knife blade or other suitable tool. If a reed tongue has been broken, the repairman must resort to a junk organ to find another one of the identical pitch. A new tongue can be made up from brass reed stock, but this is beyond the abilities of most repairmen and will not be discussed here.

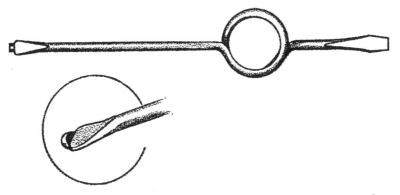

Fig. 34. A Commercially-made Reed-puller. A suitable substitute can be made by filing the proper shape in a piece of steel; often a common nail will serve satisfactorily to hook onto reeds for removal from the organ.

Occasionally, a reed will not speak even though it has sustained no damage and it has been cleaned of all dirt and dust. In this case, the reed tongue may have to be bent slightly to restore it to its speaking position. In most cases, reed tongues are bent into a rather complex curve. The free end of the tongue is sometimes given a slight sideways twist as well. It would be impossible to describe or sketch the various shapes into which the tongues are bent, as this varies from manufacturer to manufacturer and depends largely upon the tone quality which is desired from the reed. If the repairman is faced with the necessity of bending any of the reed tongues, he should remove several of the reeds close to

141

the one which must be bent, and carefully study the curvature of the tongues. He should attempt to duplicate this curvature in the tongue of the faulty reed. Generally, the tongue can be bent either upward or downward with the desired results. There will seldom be a need for sidewise bending, except in the case of reeds which speak with a buzzing sound, which is due to the side of the tongue striking the reed block as it vibrates. Experience is the best teacher in reed work, and the repairman will soon catch onto the tricks of making faulty reeds speak normally again.

Often reed organs develop sticking notes which play all the time, called ciphers. Sometimes this is caused by binding or swelling of the small rod which runs from the key to the pallet which controls the reed. In this case it is easily repaired. However, most of the time this malady is caused by trouble within the windchest, which will have to be taken apart to rectify it. Reed organ windchests are not difficult to dismantle. Usually the entire top portion of the chest, containing the reeds and other mechanism, can be taken off by removing wood screws around the edges of the chest and disconnecting any rods or other linkage which would obstruct its removal. It can often be turned over and laid on its top on a workbench, providing no loose parts drop off it in this position. When the chest has been opened, the pallet of the ciphering note should be inspected. Generally a piece of wood shaving or other foreign matter has become lodged in the pallet's leather surface, causing it to be held away from the wooden surface against which it is supposed to press, resulting in the passage of air to the reed when the pallet is closed. The matter should be removed, and if much dirt is present on the leather face of the pallet, all the pallets should be gone over with a stiff brush, to brush up the nap of the leather and remove the dirt.

Ciphers are sometimes caused by corrosion of the brass springs which return the pallets to their rest position after they have been opened by depression of the keys. These brass springs were often lubricated at the organ factories with some sort of tallow grease, which, through the years, becomes highly corrosive and deteriorates the metal of the springs. If the springs are merely corroded, but not significantly weakened, they can be cleaned and re-used. However, if some have broken, they should be replaced with new ones which can be made from spring wire or piano wire, which is locally obtainable in most areas at hardware or music stores.

Occasionally, due to climatic or other conditions, the leather facings of the pallets have loosened from the pallet surfaces and have become hard and curled. In this case, they should be replaced with white sheepskin, or heavy gasket leather if sheepskin is not handy. In most cases the old pallet leather can merely be pulled off and new leather glued on in its place.

If the repairman has occasion to dismantle the windchest of the organ, he should always check its interior for cracks. Many reed organs have been kept in warm, dry rooms, and the wood has become quite dry and brittle through the years. In numerous instances, cracking of the chest has occurred, with resulting loss of air. Every interior surface of the chest should be carefully inspected, and if cracks are discovered, strips of bellows cloth should be glued over them to make them airtight.

Before the chest is put together, the gaskets around its

edges should be checked. These should be soft enough to form airtight seals around the edges of the chest when the parts are put together. If the gaskets have hardened, new ones can be made from pieces of white gasket leather. The screws holding the chest together should be drawn up tightly, and if stripping of the threads in the wood occurs, longer screws should be inserted to create a tight seal. Any small air leaks will materially affect the performance of the organ.

All mechanical linkages should be checked for free operation, and graphite placed at any points where friction occurs. Finally, the various stops of the organ should be tested to see that they are functioning properly.

SUPPLIES

"WHAT KIND of glue do you use?" is one of the most frequently-asked questions among player piano technicians. Often individuals have widely differing techniques and methods for gluing, and disagreement is common as to what kind of glue is best for specific jobs. Some technicians will staunchly advocate the use of nothing but the so-called "white glue" on the market today, claiming that advances in chemistry have made it foolish to use anything other than the newest material. Others stick by the time-proved ground animal glue, known as "hot glue," which was used by all player piano manufacturers originally and which is satisfactory for player work, as evidenced by the fact that it is usually still holding quite tightly.

In the experience of this writer, *both* white glue and hot glue have a place in player piano rebuild work. It is strongly recommended that anyone who plans to do any large amount of player work acquires facilities for using both types of glues. White glue is valuable in situations in which the parts being glued must be aligned precisely after join-

145

ing, or in any situation in which it is undesirable for the glue to "set" quickly. White glue can generally be worked for at least five minutes after application, and in some instances this is quite desirable. For example, when applying new pneumatic cloth to striker stack pneumatics, it is the practice of this writer to use white glue. The cloth can be placed on the pneumatic surfaces unhurriedly, without fear that the glue will harden before the cloth is perfectly aligned or drawn tight. Using hot glue for this job, the repairman must work dangerously fast, and the result is sometimes faulty work. On the other hand, when gluing pneumatics back onto their decks after they have been covered, hot glue is definitely the better material. In this case, its property of rapid hardening is ideal, for it reduces clamping time by a large factor. In instances in which the two surfaces being glued can be brought together immediately after application of the glue, and before the glue has a chance to cool, hot glue is generally recommended. However, hot glue begins to harden immediately as it cools, and in applications in which there is a time lag between the application of the glue and the joining of the surfaces, white glue is generally better. Also, the repairman of today should attempt to consider the situation of the repairman of tomorrow—as there is great likelihood that forty years hence, someone else may be "re-rebuilding" the instrument. Joints which have been glued with hot glue are far easier to break apart again than are those joined with white glue. In situations in which the joints being glued will, in all likelihood, have to be broken apart again in future years, the repairman should use hot glue and thereby do the next rebuilder a favor. Hot glue possesses the undeniable disadvantage of having to be mixed and heated, two chores which make the use of white glue more convenient. However, the repairman will soon learn to anticipate his needs, and to turn on his glue pot in advance of the moment when the glue is needed. Those not wishing to assume the expense of buying an electric glue pot can get away with using an old kitchen double-boiler and a hot-plate to heat the glue mixture (do *not* heat it without a water-jacketed container). However, anyone planning on doing much player work should invest in an electric, thermostatically-controlled glue pot. A one quart thermostatic pot can be obtained from any of the piano supply houses at a cost in the twenty-dollar range.

The rebuilder must become intimately familiar with the various weights and types of pneumatic cloths. The choice of cloth can "make or break" the rebuild job, and the repairman must choose his cloth with care.

For covering striker stack pneumatics, only the very thinnest cloth should be used. When these pneumatics operate, there should be an absolute minimum of internal friction in the cloth. Cloth which is too heavy will resist the movement of the pneumatics, robbing part of their striking power.

For covering air-motors with large pneumatics, double-weight motor cloth should be used. This is a specially-made cloth for air-motors which will provide long life and no wearing at the creases. However, for smaller air-motor pneumatics, regular thin pneumatic cloth should be used. The use of this thin cloth eliminates internal friction and enables the motor to spin freely. Large motors have sufficient power to overcome this internal friction of the double-weight cloth, and in this case the heavier cloth will provide longer-lasting results. The same applies to the air-motor governor units. Both the air-motor and its governor must operate without the slightest amount of hesitation caused by internal friction within the cloth. In general, if the perimeter of the air-motor or governor pneumatic being covered is twenty inches or more, the heavier double-weight cloth should be used. For smaller pneumatics, thin cloth is suggested.

For the "accessory" pneumatics (sustaining pedal, hammer rail controls, etc.) the repairman should use "expression cloth." This is a medium double-weight cloth which will take heavier stress than the thinner cloth.

Heavy bellows cloth should be used to cover the lower bellows unit (pump and reservoir). This is usually a double layer of twill cloth fused to a thin sheet of rubber, which produces a tough and durable heavy cloth capable of withstanding high stresses.

This writer recommends the use of rubber or neoprene tubing in player piano work, rather than the plastic or vinyl favored by some technicians. (Neoprene is a synthetic rubber product, originally developed for the automotive industry, which is highly resistant to deterioration from contact with oils or greases.) Rubber or neoprene tubing is easy to use and inexpensive to purchase, in contrast to plastic tubing which is often difficult to slide onto the nipples of the player action, refuses to turn corners without pinching shut, and is sometimes more expensive than rubber. However, care must be exercised in the selection of the tubing. In general, only tubing which has been purchased from a piano supplier should be used. Some rubber tubing has a high sulphur content which causes it to crack or break down when subjected to stress. Tubing which is purchased from a supplier has normally been checked and is generally acceptable for player piano use. The tubing size for most tracker bars is $\%_{64}''$ inside diameter. The average 88-note upright piano will require between two hundred and two hundred fifty feet of tracker bar tubing unless, of course, the original was lead which does not need replacement. The most common sizes of control tubing are $\%_{16}''$, $\frac{1}{4}''$, and $\%_{8}''$, with an occasional piece of $\frac{1}{2}''$ tubing in some pianos. The size of the main supply hose varies greatly from piano to piano, and should be determined by measurement.

Pouch leather is obtainable in two types—zephir leather and tan pouch leather. Each has its own application in player work. For most pouches of diameters of one inch or larger, tan pouch leather will provide a satisfactory material. This leather is quite thin and flexible, and is very pleasant to handle and work. For smaller pouches, or for pouches which are actuated through very small tracker bar holes, zephir leather should be used. Zephir leather is one of the lightest and toughest materials available for any pneumatic application. Made from animal intestinal membrane, it provides a featherweight yet airtight pouch which will give lightning-quick action on a minimum of suction. Zephir leather is sometimes supplied with a smooth finish on one side and a slightly rougher finish on the other. When using this leather, be sure to glue the rougher side down, to insure the glue sticking fast to it. The same applies to the tan pouch leather, which should always be glued rough side down.

For re-facing valves, calf skin is recommended. This is a

tough, close-grained leather which is non-porous and which insures no leakage through the valve facing leather. For small valves, or valves which originally used very thin leather, tan pouch leather may be used. The thickness of the old valve facings should be noted, and new leather of approximately the same thickness installed.

For replacing flap valves on supply bellows, flap valve leather should be used. This is a special leather with an air-tight lacquer finish on one side and a smooth valve surface on the other.

For making gaskets, low-grade leather may be used. White alum gusset leather or any other suitable leather will do, providing it is soft enough to conform to the mating surfaces and provide a tight seal. The leather is cut to size, then glued to one side of the joint before it is assembled.

For covering the vacuum pumps of electrically-operated instruments such as reproducing pianos and nickelodeons, kangaroo skin provides an ideal substance. This is a very tough, durable leather which will outwear the heaviest rubberized cloth. If kangaroo skin is unobtainable, heavy bellows cloth may be used. For very large, heavy pumps (e. g., band organ pumps) horsehide or elk skin should be used.

The finest player piano supplies in this country are available from Player Piano Company, 620 East Douglas Avenue, Wichita, Kansas 67202. Mr. Durrell Armstrong, the owner of Player Piano Company, is an expert technician, and furnishes consistently top-grade materials at reasonable prices. He offers a very large and comprehensive selection of all types of player supplies. His catalog will be furnished upon receipt of $1.00.

SUPPLIES

Equally fine player supplies can be obtained from the following sources:

One of the oldest and most reliable sources of a general line of piano tools and supplies is Otto R. Trefz & Company, at 1305 North 27th Street, Philadelphia 19121, Pennsylvania.

The Tuners Supply Company, 94 Wheatland Street, Somerville, Massachusetts 02145 is also an old-line firm carrying a complete line of piano parts and supplies.

The Pacific Piano Supply Company is located at 11323 VanOwen Street, North Hollywood 91609. This concern not only stocks a complete line of supplies and parts, but does considerable player rebuilding work as well, with emphasis on the Ampico and the Duo-Art.

The American Piano Supply Company, Box 1055, Clifton, New Jersey 07014, one of the oldest and largest piano supply houses, has a complete line of player piano supplies, in addition to tools and parts necessary for repairing and rebuilding all types of pianos. This firm sells wholesale only to bona-fide piano technicians, dealers and manufacturers. A large profusely illustrated catalog is sent free on request, with proof of professional affiliation.

Type "A" and "G" music rolls for nickelodeons, as well as rolls for LINK pianos, are available from Edward Freyer, PO Box 373, Flemington, New Jersey 08822.

Rolls for other types of coin-pianos and nickelodeons may be obtained from the Player Piano Company cited on page 150.

Special supplies for reproducing pianos may be obtained from several suppliers throughout the country. Reprints of the Model A and B Ampico, Duo-Art, and Welte-Mignon

SUPPLIES

service manuals may be punched from The Vestal Press, 3533 Stratford Drive, Vestal, New York. The Vestal Press also furnishes complete schematic diagrams of the Model A Ampico tubing layout (the Model B Ampico diagram is contained in the service manual), as well as tubing diagrams for the Welte-Mignon and the Duo-Art. Duplicates of original factory test rolls for all three reproducing pianos may be purchased from Player Piano Company or from most of the major piano supply houses.

Readers may write to the Vestal Press, PO Box 97, Vestal, N.Y. 13850 for an up-to-date listing of suppliers. A catalog of other books in this field will also be sent on receipt of $1.00, which is refundable with any order.

Music rolls for both reproducing pianos and regular 88-note player pianos are also available from the Vestal Press, and catalogs and lists will be sent on request.

TRACKER SCALES

Model A Ampico

Starting from left:
1. Slow crescendo, bass
2. First intensity hole
3. Sustaining pedal
4. Second intensity hole
5. Fast crescendo, bass
6. Third intensity hole
7. Cancel

Starting from right:
1. Slow crescendo, treble
2. First intensity hole
3. Soft pedal
4. Second intensity hole
5. Fast crescendo, treble
6. Third intensity hole
7. Cancel
8. Rewind

Model B Ampico

Starting from left:
1. Amplifier trigger
2. Blank
3. First intensity hole
4. Sustaining pedal
5. Second intensity hole
6. Shutoff after rewind
7. Third intensity hole
8. Cancel

Starting from right:
1. Sub intensity
2. Slow crescendo
3. First intensity hole
4. Soft pedal
5. Second intensity hole
6. Fast crescendo
7. Third intensity hole
8. Cancel
9. Rewind

153

REBUILDING THE PLAYER PIANO

Duo-Art

Starting from left:
1. Rewind
2. Sustaining pedal
3. Bass theme
4. First intensity
5. Second intensity
6. Third intensity
7. Fourth intensity

Starting from right:
1. Soft pedal
2. Motor shutoff
3. Treble theme
4. First intensity
5. Second intensity
6. Third intensity
7. Fourth intensity

Welte-Mignon (Licensee and Original German)

Starting from left:
1. Mezzo-forte off
2. Mezzo-forte on
3. Crescendo off
4. Crescendo on
5. Forzando off
6. Forzando on
7. Soft pedal off
8. Soft pedal on

Starting from right:
1. Mezzo-forte off
2. Mezzo-forte on
3. Crescendo off
4. Crescendo on
5. Forzando off
6. Forzando on
7. Sustaining pedal off
8. Sustaining pedal on
9. Blank
10. Rewind

154

TRACKER SCALES

Angelus Artrio

Starting from left:
1. Intensity on accompaniment
2. Intensity on accompaniment
3. Rewind
4. Sustaining pedal
5. Bass theme
6. Intensity on accompaniment
7. Intensity on accompaniment

Starting from right:
1. First intensity on theme
2. Soft pedal
3. Second intensity on theme
4. Third intensity on theme
5. Treble theme
6. Fourth intensity on theme
7. Fifth intensity on theme

Artecho

Starting from left:
1. First intensity
2. Second intensity
3. Third intensity
4. Sustaining pedal
5. Cancel bass intensities
6. Diminuendo
7. Crescendo
8. Bass hammer rail lift

Starting from right:
1. First intensity
2. Second intensity
3. Third intensity
4. Cancel treble intensities
5. Diminuendo
6. Crescendo
7. Pianissimo
8. Treble hammer rail lift
9. Cancel for hammer rail lifts and pianissimo—long perforation, rewind

155

REBUILDING THE PLAYER PIANO

A rolls

Starting from left:
 1. Soft pedal
 2. Sustaining pedal
 3. Rewind to play
 4. Lowest playing note
61. Highest playing note
62. Additional instrument on
63. Rewind
64. Mandolin on
65. Shutoff

G rolls

Starting from left:
 1. Soft pedal
 2. Sustaining pedal
 3. Lowest playing note
27. Instrument A off
28. Rewind
29. Instrument A on
30. Snare drum
31. Instrument B on
32. Instrument B off
33. Shutoff
34. Bass drum
35. Bass drum and cymbal
36. Tympani
37. Instrument C on
38. Rewind to play
39. Instrument C off
40. Continuation of playing notes
64. Mandolin
65. Triangle

156

TRACKER SCALES

O rolls

Starting from left:

A. Rewind to play
1. Tympani
2. Bass drum and cymbal
3. Tympani
4. Indian block
5. Snare drum, single beat
6. Snare drum, roll
7. Triangle
8. Sustaining pedal
9. Soft pedal off
10. Soft pedal on
11. Mandolin off
12. Mandolin on
13. Instrument A on
14. Instrument B on
15. Percussion expression on
16. Percussion expression off
17. Instrument B off
18. Shutoff
19. Instrument A off
20. Lowest playing note
86. Tambourine
87. Automatic swell (used only in large Coinola)
88. Crash cymbal (used only in large Coinola)
B. Rewind

157

REBUILDING THE PLAYER PIANO

M rolls

A. Chain perforations, no apparent purpose
B. Rewind to play
C. Chain perforations, control automatic tune selector
1. Shutoff
2. Purpose not known
3. Soft pedal on
4. Soft pedal off
5. Triangle
6. Swell shutters on
7. Swell shutters off
8. Snare drum
9. Instrument A on
10. Instrument A off
11. Tympani
12. Bass drum
13. Tympani
14. Instrument B on
15. Instrument B off
16. Instrument C on
17. Instrument C off
18. Instrument D on
19. Instrument D off
20. Mandolin on
21. Mandolin off
22. Sustaining pedal
23. Tambourine
24. Castanet
25. Lowest playing note
88. Highest playing note
D. Same as C
E. Rewind
F. Same as A

TRACKER SCALES

Link RX and C rolls

Starting from left (back of piano):
1. Soft off
2. Soft on
3. Xylophone on
4. Sustaining pedal
5. Lowest playing note
66. Shutoff
67. Teed in with hole 3, xylophone on
68. Mandolin on
69. Mandolin and xylophone off
70. Blank

159

Link A rolls

Starting from left (back of piano):
 1. Soft off
 2. Soft on
 3. Blank
 4. Sustaining pedal
 5. Tambourine
 6. Left beater on snare drum
 7. Center beater on snare drum
 8. Right beater on snare drum
 9. Triangle
10. Tom-tom
11. Right beater on wood block
12. Left beater on wood block
13. Front pipes on
14. Release for both pipes
15. Rear pipes on
16. Triangle or bass drum
17. Lowest playing note
66. Shutoff
67. Mandolin on
68. Mandolin off
69. Blank
70. Blank

Wurlitzer 65-Note Player Piano Tracker Layout

1. Coin trip.
2. Soft pedal and mandolin on.
3. Soft pedal and mandolin off.
4. Sustaining pedal on.
5. Sustaining pedal off.
6. Snare drum.

7 to 71. Chromatic scale, 65 notes from A to C sharp.
(Middle C is tracker hole no. 35)

72. (See explanation below)
73. (See explanation below)
74. Bass drum, triangle, cymbal.
75. Rewind.

Controls are as follows:

Case 1. Piano with mandolin and one extra instrument (such as either a rank of violin pipes or a rank of flute pipes). Hole no.72 turns the extra instrument off; no. 73 turns it on.

Case 2. Piano with mandolin and two instruments (two ranks of pipes). Hole no. 72 turns the first rank off and the second rank on. Hole 73 turns the first rank on and the second rank off. (Note that both ranks cannot be on at the same time; also one rank must be on at all times).

Case 3. Piano with mandolin, two ranks of pipes and bells. The pipes are controlled as in Case 2 above. The bells are controlled by a multiplexing arrangement involving holes 2, 3, 4, and 5 (which, separately, have other functions as noted in the above layout). The bells are turned on when holes 4 and 5 are used together. Both holes appear side by side on the roll. Note that holes 4 and 5 normally operate the sustaining pedal on the piano. After turning the bells on the longer of the two slots (of holes 4 and 5) will determine whether the pedal is on or off. The bells are turned off by holes 2 and 3 appearing at the same time. The longer of the two slots will determine the position of the soft pedal and mandolin.

Case 4. Piano with mandolin, two ranks of pipes, bells, and xylophone (This is an exceedingly rare situation: only a few 65-note orchestrions were built with xylophones). In this instance the pipes are controlled as in Case 2, the bells are controlled as in Case 3 and the xylophone is operated as follows: The xylophone turns on when holes 72 and 73 are open at the same time (the two slots appearing side by side on the roll). Note that these holes usually control the pipe registers. The xylophone is turned off with holes 2 and 3 — the same as with the bells in Case 3 above.

Note: Instruments with bells or xylophone or both have either a special shuttle valve or a special valve assembly for the multiplexing as described in Cases 3 and 4.

WurliTzer 65-note information supplied by courtesy of Hathaway and Bowers, 11975 E. Florence, Santa Fe Springs, California 90670

REBUILDING THE PLAYER PIANO

Seeburg H rolls

Starting from left:
1. Soft pedal
2. Sustaining pedal
3. Lowest bass note
35. Flutes off
36. Flutes on
37. Rewind
38. Violins off
39. Violins on
40. Solo off
41. Solo on
42. Rewind to play
43. Xylophone off
44. Shutoff
45. Xylophone on
46. Castanets
47. Full vacuum to stack
48. Low vacuum to stack
49. Snare drum
50. Bass drum and cymbal
51. Tympani
52. Tympani
53. Continuation of playing notes
87. Mandolin
88. Triangle

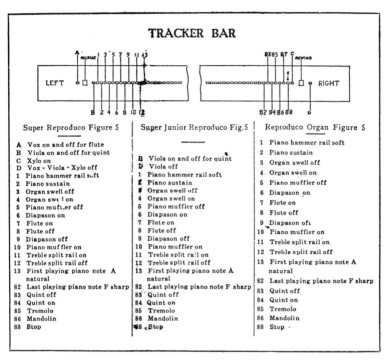

TRACKER BAR

Super Reproduco Figure 5	Super Junior Reproduco Fig.5	Reproduco Organ Figure 5
		1 Piano hammer rail soft
A Vox on and off for flute		2 Piano sustain
B Viola on and off for quint		3 Organ swell off
C Xylo on	B Viola on and off for quint	4 Organ swell on
D Vox - Viola - Xylo off	D Viola off	5 Piano muffler off
1 Piano hammer rail soft	1 Piano hammer rail soft	6 Diapason on
2 Piano sustain	2 Piano sustain	7 Flute on
3 Organ swell off	3 Organ swell off	8 Flute off
4 Organ swell on	4 Organ swell on	9 Diapason off
5 Piano muffler off	5 Piano muffler off	10 Piano muffler on
6 Diapason on	6 Diapason on	11 Treble split rail on
7 Flute on	7 Flute on	12 Treble split rail off
8 Flute off	8 Flute off	13 First playing piano note A
9 Diapason off	9 Diapason off	natural
10 Piano muffler on	10 Piano muffler on	82 Last playing piano note F sharp
11 Treble split rail on	11 Treble split rail on	83 Quint off
12 Treble split rail off	12 Treble split rail off	84 Quint on
13 First playing piano note A	13 First playing piano note A	85 Tremolo
natural	natural	86 Mandolin
82 Last playing piano note F sharp	82 Last playing piano note F sharp	88 Stop ·
83 Quint off	83 Quint off	
84 Quint on	84 Quint on	
85 Tremolo	85 Tremolo	
86 Mandolin	86 Mandolin	
88 Stop	88 Stop	

Reproduco Piano-Pipe Organ

(manufactured by Operators Piano Company)

From *ENOUGH TIME;* copyright Time, Inc., 1959.